COMMANDO MINDSET

Ben Williams is a former Royal Marines Commando with over a decade of experience. He served in Afghanistan and has trained Commando recruits. Williams has also founded a coaching and performance business, Vanguard Global Solutions, that trains high-profile clients in elite businesses within industries such as global banking, vehicle manufacturing and the music industry, as well as professional sporting outfits, including the England football team.

COMMANDO MINDSET

Find Your Motivation, Realize Your Potential, Achieve Your Goals

BEN WILLIAMS

BUSINESS

PENGUIN BUSINESS

UK | USA | Canada | Ireland | Australia
India | New Zealand | South Africa

Penguin Business is part of the Penguin Random House group of companies
whose addresses can be found at global.penguinrandomhouse.com.

First published 2020

001

Copyright © Ben Williams, 2020

Design by Mónica Oliveira

The moral right of the copyright holder has been asserted

Set in 12/14.75pt Dante MT Std
Typeset by Jouve (UK), Milton Keynes
Printed and bound in Great Britain by Clays Ltd, Elcograf S.p.A.

A CIP catalogue record for this book is available from the British Library

ISBN: 978-0-241-41605-1

Follow us on LinkedIn: linkedin.com/company/penguinbusiness

www.greenpenguin.co.uk

To my wonderful wife Natalie and
my two beautiful children, Zachary and Layla.

Thank you for being the inspiration
that drives my courage
and forces me to act.

Uncle Adrian, much loved and sorely missed.

CONTENTS

MY STORY

*A journey of a thousand miles
starts with a single step.*
Lao Tzu

**Afghanistan,
Wednesday, 24 August 2011**

It's five o'clock in the morning. In our order of march, we're ushered towards an old gate at the front of the compound. Wearing the most up-to-date equipment and clutching our advanced weaponry, we brace ourselves for another long and intense patrol.

We are Seven Troop, Lima Company. I'm third man from the front; there's a dog handler, his furry companion and then Jordan in front of me. Our commander, Vicey, is behind, followed by Darlo, Gav, Spence, the remainder of the twelve-man patrol and Vicky, our medic. All of the patrol – my colleagues and friends – are willing to lay down their lives for each other at the drop of a hat.

The tour so far has been bloody and 'kinetic', a term marines use to describe intense action in battle. Yesterday, six of our men were injured in the first two hours after reaching the target location. And the rest of the day was spent fighting ferociously. Our closest friends are being killed and maimed by a relentless, invisible enemy and it's starting to take its toll on everyone.

This morning, minutes pass by like seconds. The air is thick with silence broken only occasionally by birds chirping above. If Afghanistan hadn't become a country of war and terror, it would be a nice place to visit sometime, I think to myself. As it was many years ago, when the Beatles made it popular in the UK. But today, under copious amounts of body armour, I'm sweating profusely in the rapidly rising heat.

The knotting within my stomach intensifies.

This routine is normal for us: waking early, eating rations for breakfast and readying ourselves for another patrol. Always hoping for the best, yet expecting the worst. But something is different today.

The marines seem quieter than usual, perhaps unnerved by the events of yesterday. Their silence amplifies the tension in the air.

I feel something bad is looming.

Our watching sentries on the roof give us the thumbs up. The immediate area is safe. The rusty old gate needs wrenching open, resisting our departure, as if trying to tell us to stay in the compound. We step out across a path. We're out on patrol.

Straightaway, there's an obstacle. An irrigation ditch. In Afghanistan, irrigation ditches can be high-banked, two to three metres deep, full of water and mud. It often takes one or two guys to help someone cross. Twelve men and our female medic have to take it in turns to struggle in and out. Slowing the patrol right down, making us vulnerable.

On this tour, already many marines from the company and our unit, 42 Commando, have been blown up and lost limbs from stepping into such ditches. Placing improvised explosive devices (IEDs) in the ground, at a point where we are struggling and at our slowest, is a preferred tactic of our hidden enemy. So we always have a point man at the front, responsible for clearing a path for us everywhere we go. Checking for IEDs and booby traps.

Today, no issues so far. The point man, Jordan, turns around and gives the nod. The rest of the patrol starts slowly across. We help each other pull our heavily laden selves out of the ditch. We cross successfully without problem. The only cost is time. Once the last man is ready, we move off.

Our target location is a compound in the village nearby – ten to twelve houses no more than 350 metres from the compound we occupied yesterday. Its rooftops are visible from ours.

Our aim is to tell the locals of our intentions in the area. To inform them that we're here to help and protect them. However, this village is situated in an area of continuous Taliban activity. Convincing the villagers of their safety is going to be tough.

During the lull in yesterday's battle, another patrol entered the village to sweep through, check it for traces of enemy activity and begin reassuring the villagers. They encountered little response from the locals and no sign of the enemy. Maybe we'll have more luck.

Leaving the irrigation ditch behind us, we enter a cornfield at the height of its crop. Our vision is limited to a metre, if that. The heat is sweltering. Moisture from the vegetation adds a humid burden. We long to stop, take a knee, look at the ground and just breathe. We can't. We must stay switched on and vigilant, ready for the enemy's next move.

Any firefight in this environment will be close proximity, just metres apart and deadly.

Moving through is extremely hard work. Every corn stalk catches and snags on our kit. But we press on. This field has to end soon.

Exiting the field is going to bring us out onto a dusty dirt track, no more than fifty metres from the entrance to the village. Low walls are on both sides, enclosing more cornfields. Leading up towards the village, the track is crossed by another right next to the compound we need to enter.

Jordan halts and takes a knee. He's assessing the dangers of moving onto the track. The rest of the patrol waits in the intense humidity of the cornfield.

Jordan is a twenty-year-old marine now charged with the safety of us all. As point man, he's empowered by our commander to judge the atmospherics and make decisions of huge responsibility. All to ensure we're not wandering into an ambush or any other surprise the Taliban want to hit us with.

This type of assessment is the norm. Allowing Commander Paul 'Vicey' Vice, our extremely experienced and formidable leader, to use his senses and gauge the atmosphere of the area with Jordan.

Right now, however, something feels different. The atmosphere is strange and the hairs on our necks are bristling. Yet, nothing's happening, there's nobody around.

Knowing the dangers, Vicey decides to continue the patrol and start moving up the track. We have a professional job to do. We're here as elite Royal Marines Commandos, unperturbed by the enemy's ruthless tactics. Following commanders like Vicey, who make critical battle-winning decisions time and time again, we trust their every command, no matter the danger.

We move a few metres along the track. A tractor passes through the junction we're approaching. The driver sees us and floors it – as best as you can accelerate a tractor away from a group of heavily armed marines.

Jordan and I are now no further than twenty metres from the junction. As we near it, two men appear, dressed in black clothing and trainers – a typical Taliban outfit. We're as surprised to see them as they are to see us. Startled, we lock eyes before they run off into the field to our right.

We're not sent to Afghanistan to shoot and kill unarmed people. Even though we know they're more than likely Taliban, there's nothing we can do. But alarm bells are ringing. Something is imminent and we must react.

'Quick get up to the compound, now!' Vicey commands, urging us to move on.

I take a few steps, then the earth explodes around us with an almighty bang. The huge explosion rips through me, showering me in dirt and dust, shrapnel, mud and rocks. An immediate blistering heat burns my skin. I'm hit extremely hard in the head by something that my helmet deflects. My left calf is instantly a source of pain. A lot of pain.

This happens in a second: the noise, the burning, the pain. It's so quick that I'm left standing, almost unmoved, shocked by the impact and surprise of what has just happened. But not for long. In one more second I drop to the ground, gripping my calf to squeeze off the pain that isn't subsiding.

I am completely unable to assess anyone else or my own

injuries. My vision is orange from the dust, dirt and smoke that hang in the air, blinding me like a storm on Mars. I can hear nothing but muffled noises and the high-pitched ringing, as my senses try to comprehend what has just happened. My head is concussed from the impact of the explosion.

The first faculty to return is smell: cordite, explosives and subtle hints of burning flesh, a concoction of scents I will never forget.

Waking up to the reality of the scene, I remember I'm not the only one here. *What about the lads?* I think, a worry that briefly numbs the pain in my leg. I find myself aimlessly crawling around, desperately searching for my mates, trying to listen out to anything I can.

All I hear is muffled shouts and screams. Then, a gust of wind clears the smoke and dust and I see a sight that will stay etched on my mind for the rest of my life. Unconscious bodies lie all over the track. Clothes ripped, blood everywhere, weapons and equipment blown to pieces. Lifeless friends lying still on the ground upon which they just trod.

Within seconds, the remaining members of the patrol are sprinting towards us, risking everything to save the lives of those fighting death.

Lying only metres away from me is Vicey, unconscious. He's bleeding from an artery in his neck, which a piece of shrapnel has severed. My commander, our leader whom we all see as invincible, is lying in the middle of a dusty Afghan village, his life slipping away. He's the guy who has got us out of countless situations others would have failed in. We have become his ever dutiful and trusting followers. Only a few days ago, he won the Military Cross for his bravery in battle.

Trying to pull my injured leg back to life, I witness marine Richy Pencott sprint and kneel on Vicey's neck, controlling the bleed that's killing him. He's saving the life of our leader, but needs more help.

Richy switches his knee for his hands, struggling to reach for the clotting agent in his medical kit to pack into Vicey's wound and stop the bleeding.

I drag myself over to them both. Without speaking, I take my own clotting agent from my med kit and pass it to him. Richy and I switch roles. I place my fingers in Vicey's neck as Richy begins unwrapping the packaging before stuffing it into the wound. Vicky, our medic, races to us and takes over, pushing me aside so she can concentrate on saving our commander.

All I can do is lie there next to Vicey, wounded alongside my leader, gripping his hand and telling him to hold on for his family.

As all our casualties, including me, are being stretchered to the landing zone for evacuation, firing begins overhead. The roar of helicopters fills the air. An Apache Longbow attack helicopter is engaging Taliban insurgents, swooping in low, devastating the treeline near us with its 30mm cannon.

Throughout this, Richy, Vicky and the remainder of Seven Troop stay with the casualties and ensure we get to safety.

That day, 24 August 2011, changed my life for ever.

Working in unison with commanders and young men through an extremely difficult situation changed how I perceived leadership and strength of mind.

I'd experienced men and women acting way above their pay scales to ensure no further harm or death came to the rest of Seven Troop.

Colleagues like Richy put everything at risk to ensure the lives of Vicey, Darlo and everyone else were preserved, even if it meant risking his own.

Richy saved the life of our commander, not out of duty but out of faith. He did it both with courage and by using another amazing attribute: the Commando mindset.

COMMANDO TO COACH

Six years later, in 2017, I found myself standing in a small wood in Devon, proudly wearing my green beret, now a leader myself.

Overseeing a group of tired people fumbling around with military kit, I was discussing leadership, performance and how new cultures can be installed within teams. Tall and athletically built, my partner in the conversation folded his arms, then reached for his chin to stroke his stubble in a contemplative manner.

That group of fumbling people was the senior England men's football team. The man with me, stroking his stubble, was Gareth Southgate, the team's manager.

The group had joined us at the Commando training centre, Lympstone, for a weekend of assault courses, team building and some basic military training. For the players and staff, it was an opportunity to take part in activities a little different from what they were used to, something outside the norm. But, for Gareth, it was an opportunity to test character, build a culture and instil leadership – three fundamental attributes required in creating a successful team.

World Cup 2018 in Russia was just over a year away and England had yet to qualify. Gareth wanted to embed and nurture a culture within the team that few had seen before and take it into the World Cup finals and beyond.

Encouraging the players to develop a mindset of maturity and professionalism, Gareth was trying to expel the prima donna behaviour footballers are sometimes associated with. He was changing the way his players acted and were therefore perceived. He had a dramatic impact on the team, one that would lead to England's most successful World Cup in twenty-eight years while simultaneously bringing the nation behind them.

What a turn of events!

Standing in that wood deep in conversation, I had little idea that, after the tournament, I'd receive a call from Gareth's manager informing me that my company, Vanguard Global Solutions, was to be involved in a special event to be held by the Football Writers' Association in his honour.

If the invitation left me feeling bewildered and a little bit overwhelmed, that was nothing compared with the event itself. I was invited to the Savoy hotel in London, to join Gareth, along with a plethora of sporting legends. Not only that, but I was to personally deliver the FWA Tribute Award speech to the man himself!

Come the day in the cold January of 2019, my wife Natalie and I took our seats at the top table. As the remaining 400 guests applauded Gareth and our entry into the room, we were like two giddy children. Joining us at the table were key figures in football, most notably *Match of the Day* host Gary Lineker and his son George.

As the finest food was laid before us, the wine flowed – at least into my wife's glass. All a far cry from the dusty compounds and rations in Helmand Province. However, my wine glass stayed empty and my stomach tightly locked as I nervously sipped some fizzy water. Thoughts were racing around my head and I found myself checking my speech time and again. Not only to ensure it was in order, but also to make sure I was as prepared as possible – I didn't want to make myself look a complete fool in front of such an audience.

When it was time for the speeches, Gary Lineker took to the stage and addressed the room with a wonderfully powerful and insightful speech, celebrating Gareth's career to date. My nervousness was amplified even more when Gary told a joke about waistcoats, one that I had planned to use. 'Shit, shit, shit!' I repeated to my wife. 'Lineker's used my joke!'

My wife was as calm as ever, perhaps helped by the wine. Quietly speaking into my ear, she comforted me. 'Calm down, you've worked so hard, you deserve to be here. Just relax and be yourself.' Natalie was right. It suddenly dawned on me how different my life – our lives – had become.

I had taken myself from being a broke, suicidal drug addict to someone who had just completed ten years' service as a Royal Marines Commando. Now, I was about to step on stage before a glittering audience and deliver a tribute speech for one of England's most successful football managers ever. Players and icons that I watched and admired as a child were about to listen to me speak about culture, leadership and mindset.

I had got myself to this position by hard work, determination, desire and, most importantly, belief. I had dared to dream, gained a focus and chased my goals with a ruthless tenacity until I achieved them.

Through this, I found reward and success. And I was still only thirty-one.

So, how did I do it?

I achieved all this by living and breathing a Commando mindset. A mindset I have later come to understand that I owned well before I ever set foot in the Royal Marines.

An unusual start to life

There's no denying that joining the marines changed my life. In fact, it actually saved my life.

Before I found my path in the marines, I spent my teenage years locked in a bitter and twisted cycle of isolation, depression and anger. Before I reached my teens, I witnessed my parents' very difficult separation. I moved home and school six times. I graded averagely at school and had zero qualifications. I was bullied. I became addicted to cocaine, steroids and several other drugs. I had no purpose or ambition and no plan for the future. I felt lost, not knowing what I would do next, and I felt trapped, locked in a maelstrom of low self-esteem and destructive behaviour. After leaving school at sixteen, I witnessed extreme violence while working as a nightclub bouncer, then I witnessed the death of a nightclubber right before my eyes. I was exposed to a lot of tough experiences few deal with at such a young age but I had also brought on a lot of my problems all by myself. I was ashamed of who I had become. On several occasions, I questioned the point of living. At twenty, I felt worthless.

Twenty

So, what does a person think when they feel they have nothing left? End it! Take myself out of the equation and rid myself of the misery. When I look back, I realize that was a completely selfish attitude. Despite some of the bad, I had lots of good things going for me. A wonderful girlfriend, supportive family and some great friends. But, at the time, I just couldn't see it.

One day, back in early 2008, I decided to kill myself. I didn't know how, with what or where, but I knew that enough was enough. Then, later that week, I happened to see on YouTube a TV commercial for the Royal Marines from 2001. Fate works in mysterious ways.

In the advert, a young recruit is seen running through waist-deep bogs and crawling through muddy tunnels while fighting extreme exhaustion. His impressive appearance, equipment, rifle and sheer determination – all of it captivated me.

At one obstacle, the picture freezes with the words, *What's your limit?*

The young man progresses and fights on through a fully submerged tunnel, getting his leg caught along the way, trapping him beneath the surface.

Is it here?

When he frees himself, he exits the water, inhaling deeply, and then the image freezes again.

Here?

The picture holds slightly longer.

Yes? Don't even fill in the form.

Then, as an ORC (Offshore Raiding Craft) traverses the screen in the dark of night, the young man sports the famous green beret as he moves towards his target.

Freezing again, the well-known motto appears . . .

99.99% need not apply.

No music or dramatic speeches. Just the intense call to action.

When the advert finished, the words stayed etched in my mind. I wondered whether I might be one of the 0.01% they were looking for. As a boy, it had always been my desire to earn the green beret – to become a Commando. However, somewhere along the way, I had lost that vision. The dream had fizzled out and become nothing but a distant memory. I had gone from imagining being a Royal Marine as a young hopeful lad to wanting to kill myself as an unemployed drug addict.

That advert saved my life. Like a light bulb, something switched in my head the very moment the young Royal Marine left the screen. My attitude changed, as did my mindset from that moment onwards.

That year, I applied for the Royal Marines and completely turned my life around. I avoided taking the easy option of ending my life, saving my family the heartbreak and grieving I would have inevitably caused, and instead began fulfilling a once distant dream, working incredibly hard to transform my lot.

The marines changed me as a person. My military career showed me who I am and took me from despair to repair. In the marines, my life was stripped back to the basics and was then rebuilt afresh. At the end of my training I was equipped with the tools, knowledge and skills of one of the world's elite fighting forces.

Through my training, I discovered that, before I could ever attempt to lead anyone else, I would first need to effectively lead myself.

Understanding this helped me realize that I had owned a Commando mindset before I stepped foot in the military. To change myself from a drug addict contemplating suicide to someone in the right mental and physical shape to even apply for the Commandos, let alone be accepted for and complete the training, took immense courage and determination.

Just over a decade has passed since that day I considered taking my own life. Having served my country under the renowned green beret, my work as a business and performance coach now leads me around the

UK, sometimes around the world, meeting new people and helping them unlock their potential. Whether I am working with an organization or individuals like yourself, my sole purpose is to help you develop your skills and find success. And that is what *Commando Mindset* is about. This book draws heavily upon the lessons, ethos, values and spirit of my beloved Royal Marines. But it also draws on my personal experiences before I joined them and my work as a coach after I left.

So, why listen to me?

You may be wondering what makes my voice the one you should listen to in order to help you find your potential, achieve your goals and strive for something you feel is beyond your limits.

Yes, I've won medals, but plenty of other war veterans have won more. I haven't spent years at university studying performance, nor am I a psychologist who has dedicated his life to studying mindsets.

Instead, I am someone who has started right at the bottom, alone, with only a feeling of worthlessness to keep me company. But I turned it around and climbed to the top, achieving things far beyond what I ever thought possible – achievements that came to fruition only because I believed in myself and challenged myself.

Being a Royal Marines Commando put me alongside some of the most inspiring leaders and determined colleagues and friends. I was surrounded by highly motivated people who were always striving for excellence – which, as it turns out, is extremely infectious.

As a result, I gained a wealth of experience I now realize that anyone can use, both in or out of the military. Being a Commando made me a better family man, friend, business owner, consultant and coach. It allowed me access to a new world of possibility.

I want to share all that I learned so that you too can experience a journey like mine and fulfil your potential. I hope that *Commando Mindset* will reach people around the world. Whether you're daunted by impending exams, trying for a baby, creating a start-up, growing a business, applying for a new job, doing your first marathon, attempting Everest, moving industries, or gaining leadership responsibilities for the first time – *Commando Mindset* will help you. In these pages you'll find valuable lessons to help you achieve success, no matter what challenges you face, no matter where you come from.

In life, we often feel as if we're being held back by something, whether that's by a specific situation we're in, by others or – most of the time – by ourselves. However, it's never too late to make a difference. You own the ability to change and succeed in anything you put your mind to.

My journey has made me realize that we *all* have a Commando mindset beneath our layers of self-doubt and fear. That winning attitude is in there somewhere, we just need to unleash it.

This book will be the catalyst for *your* journey to success.

By gaining a Commando mindset, you WILL succeed. You'll discover a wealth of purpose. You'll believe in yourself. You will endure hardship. You will struggle. And you will achieve your goals.

Now it's time to take a breath, a step back, as we look first at what it means to be a Commando and then what a Commando mindset comprises.

WHAT IT MEANS TO BE A COMMANDO

Commando (noun) A member of an elite light-infantry or special forces organization, often specializing in amphibious landings, parachuting and abseiling; a soldier trained to make raids and assaults; an operator of unconventional warfare.

The word 'Commando' was used by Afrikaner guerrillas during the Second Boer War, 1899–1902, the title assigned to combat units which played a specific role. By 1942, the word had become permanently established within Britain's military, as the British Commandos were born as part of the Royal Marines.

The Royal Marines are steeped in over 350 years of illustrious history, full of immeasurable acts of heroism, courage, leadership and sacrifice.

Owning invaluable skills, Commandos have seen action in every conflict since World War II, all the way through to Iraq and Afghanistan. They now stand tall as one of the world's most impressive and experienced elite fighting forces, capable of deploying anywhere on the planet at a moment's notice – from the Arctic Circle to searing deserts, dense jungles to teeming cities. The marines are not only ready and prepared but also willing.

Once a marine, always a marine

We Commandos own an ethos that drives us and provides us with a precise way of thinking:

- *Be the first to understand; the first to adapt and respond; and the first to overcome.*

As part of the Commando mindset, this way of thinking is fundamental in ensuring we are prepared for every mission, challenge and operation.

Our values are simple, but powerful:

- *Excellence,* strive to do better
- *Integrity,* tell the truth
- *Self-discipline,* resist the easy option
- *Humility,* respect the rights, diversity and values of others.

And our spirits are equally profound:

- *Courage,* get out front and do what is right
- *Determination,* never give up
- *Unselfishness,* friends first, team second, self last
- *Cheerfulness,* make humour the heart of morale.

These values have forged the Commandos' unique spirit and way of being: capable of immeasurable strength, courage and fortitude to complete any task.

Special

Royal Marines Commandos train hard, owning physical strength and fitness capable of sustaining us within inhospitable environments for months on end, often against a ruthless enemy.

We are a special breed, priding ourselves on our diligence and eye for detail, tenacious discipline, immense accountability and an unrelenting persistence to see out every mission to the very end.

Due to the high standards to which Commandos are trained and operate, the Royal Marines provide over 60 per cent of manpower to all UK Special Forces regiments.

UK Special Forces (UKSF)

I am personally in awe of our British special forces. I find their secrecy irresistible and their audacious operations captivating. At one stage in my career, my ambition was to join them. Unfortunately, due to an injury that affected my hearing, that never happened.

Through recent TV programmes and chart-topping books, the curtain has been lifted on the elusive SAS (Special Air Service) and SBS (Special Boat Service). Personalities such as Andy McNab, Chris Ryan, Ant Middleton and Jason Fox have captivated millions with their displays of unparalleled endurance and their impressive mindsets. Yet the question many people are left asking after watching programmes such as *SAS: Who Dares Wins* is: 'How do they become who they are?'

I've talked at length with operators from across UKSF – many of whom I regard as close friends – posing the question time and time again: 'What makes you the best?' And, so often, I've been met with the same answer, and a humbling one, too: the values they learned at the elite organizations such as the Royal Marines Commandos and Army Parachute Regiment, where they first began crafting their mindset.

Who becomes a Commando?

During over a decade's service in the military I've had ample opportunity to reflect on what makes a Royal Marine. I've always been fascinated by the programming of a Commando. I've taken the time to sit with neurologists, psychologists and other experts to explore new answers, trying to understand whether there's a distinct difference between us and anyone outside our elite culture.

I've wondered whether it's the physicality and intensity of training, or something far superior, deep within our being.

My conclusion? There *is* something deep within every Commando that makes us who we are. And that's a unique mindset:

- Commandos adopt psychological processes that don't allow us to take the easy option or get comfortable.
- Commandos aren't worried by failure, using it as an opportunity to learn and grow.
- Commandos own a tenacious ability to ensure we see out every mission, enduring the toughest challenges and difficult situations until we succeed.

INTRODUCING THE COMMANDO MINDSET

At the start of my military career I thought Royal Marines were different, that we were superior to every other military outfit and far more capable than any civilian. However, I soon began to think differently.

<u>I realized that every single one of us – civilian or Commando – owns the ability to unlock an elite way of thinking and being.</u>

I adopted a winning mindset long before I arrived at the gates of the Commando training centre. Like me, those who joined the Commandos had already activated their elite mindset. A mindset that, when combined with the ethos, values and spirit of the Royal Marines, created a unique person who could go far beyond what many would deem possible.

The only difference I now see between us and you is that we solved the equation early.

In my case, before I joined the military, I had to discipline myself and get clean from drugs. I needed to disconnect myself from the violent lifestyle that had embroiled me. I had to face inner demons to get me to my fittest. To achieve all this I had to awaken a mindset that had lain dormant for years.

I believe this mindset is in all of us. All you need to do is to discover and adopt it and it will help you achieve any dream, ambition or goal that you may have. But you have to adopt this mindset now – not tomorrow, but today.

Hang on, what's a mindset?

So, what's a mindset? And what the hell is a *Commando* mindset?

Is a mindset the way in which we are programmed to think?
Can a mindset be calculated, viewed or assessed?
Does having a particular mindset lead to failure or success?
Can we change our mindsets?

In the *Oxford English Dictionary*, the word mindset is described as 'a set of attitudes or fixed ideas that somebody has and that are often difficult to change'. So, more questions . . .

If a mindset is described in relation to attitudes, does this then
    denote a settled way of thinking or feeling about something?
Does a mindset simply reflect a person's attitude on a given day?
Do we all possess completely different mindsets?

Every person owns many individual and varied attitudes and beliefs. You only need to look at your family and friends to witness how varied they can be.

We all regularly experience feelings of high and low motivation that dictate the course of our lives. If you wake up tired after a rough night's sleep, you're unlikely to feel highly motivated and inspired for work – possibly claiming you're not in the 'right mindset'.

Yes, it is common for our mindset to shift regularly, creating imbalance and unfocused decisions, because we just don't *feel* in the right frame of mind.

After a full-on day in the office, coming home to a bottle of wine and dinner seems far more appealing then heading out into a cold night of rain and pain on a 10k training run for your upcoming marathon.

<u>The easy option is far more appealing than the difficult, yet it is the difficult that carries far greater reward – and this is what those with a Commando mindset see.</u>

Which mindset do you have?

In the past few decades, many psychologists have studied thinking patterns and human behaviour to try to pinpoint what mindset is and how we control it.

Research conducted by Dr Carol Dweck – published in her 2006 book *Mindset* – identifies two mindset behaviours: *fixed* and *growth*.

A *fixed* mindset represents those who avoid challenge and give up early on obstacles. They view both effort and criticism with a negative eye and may feel threatened by the success of others. They may plateau early in life and not reach their full potential, often conforming to a more deterministic view of the world. They would rather look good than try to be good.

A *growth* mindset is characterized by a more development-focused way of thinking. It's evident when people embrace challenge and persist through obstacles. Effort is the route towards mastery and criticism is feedback filled with many lessons. Someone with a growth mindset finds inspiration in the success of others, and is far more likely to be fulfilled in life. They might also have a greater sense of free will.

Dweck also highlights that people's mindsets are often a com-
bination of the two. You may find you have a growth mindset in
some situations and a fixed mindset in others.

Think about your own life: which are the fixed-mindset areas
and which are the growth-mindset ones?

What do I think?

For me, mindset is the mental state of a person at any particular time –
their 'frame of mind'.

Mindsets can *easily* fluctuate. One day you may be in a good
frame of mind and another not so much. If you are hungry, tired and
dehydrated, your mental state is going to be poorer than someone
who is full, well rested and watered. Your physiological being affects
your mental state, just as much as your attitude does. If one day
you awake pumped and the next you're flat, you might be switching between a fixed and growth mindset depending on what went
on in your life the day before. Of course, this is normal. Even I fluctuate between mindsets sometimes. I am human, after all! But the
goal is to increase how often your mindset is positive – be it growth
or Commando.

I believe that, if a person owns a greater sense of awareness in *how*
and *why* they are thinking and feeling as they are, then they own the
ability to change their mindset there and then, on the spot.

**Psychologists call this 'metacognition': the ability to think
about thinking, a conscious and deliberate process in which
you analyse and manipulate your thought processes to solve
problems and to achieve a task.**

I am thinking about noticing.
I am thinking about wondering.

I am thinking about seeing.
I am thinking about feeling.

If we're aware of our thoughts, we're more able to turn our negative thoughts into positive ones.

I'm feeling down; I need to pick myself up.
I don't feel like doing it, but I should do it anyway.
I want to achieve my goal; I will achieve my goal!

Throughout this book, I'm going to help you turn your negative thinking into positive thinking. I'm going to help you develop a winning mindset so you can stop holding yourself back and chase your dreams.

Commando Mindset isn't a course of instructions to go outside and crawl through mud, run over hills, shout at your staff or take out your enemy.

Commando Mindset is going to help you develop a state of mind to achieve something that you felt was once beyond your capabilities.

For my fellow marines and me, the Commando mindset symbolizes who and what we are – the power to push through when all others fail.

How this book will help you

The Royal Marines have an exemplary leadership culture and their strongest spirit is unselfishness. The Commando mindset is built around unselfishness, putting others first before ourselves, creating a group of people that not only lead, but inspire each other.

In *Commando Mindset*, I will help you unlock the strength of mind that has carried so many people like myself further than we thought possible.

The book will encourage you to reflect on your drive, ambition and goals and highlight new areas of growth. It will require you to be honest with yourself and work out what you stand for and want from life.

I will draw on teachings and principles I learned in the marines, using stories of training and combat to help bring my concepts to life.

Alongside this, I will use models and frameworks that I have developed as a business consultant and performance coach since leaving the military.

Combining experiences and teachings of the military with my own methodologies, I will be your guide to success.

THE ICE MODEL

To help you get there, I'm going to share a model I developed called the ICE model. It's made up of three distinct parts I think it's essential you work on to achieve your goals – Inspiration, Courage and Enactment.

- Inspiration will help you unearth what truly drives you . . .
  are you inspired by a role model? Friend or family? A tangible
  object? Values? Or, simply money? We all have something
  that inspires us to act and that spurs us on when we are facing
  tough challenges. Our inspiration might be something we
  dream of achieving or reaching. And our inspiration can
  change, move, evolve or be reinvented. But, at any given point,
  we all always need inspiration to keep us moving forward.
- Courage looks at turning your inspiration into something
  more . . . Bringing it to life means being able to push through
  doubt and challenge, adversity and pain. Courage is what's
  required to move out of the comfort zone and take that leap.
  To have courage, you must first have belief in yourself. You
  must believe in yourself so deeply that you're pulled towards
  your goals or ambitions. Belief and courage will carry you
  through fear and doubt. Harnessing your courage will keep
  you attached to the path of success.
- Enactment will challenge you to act . . . You can have all
  the inspiration and courage in the world, but if you aren't
  willing to act, then your goals and ambitions will remain only

dreams. When we try to act on a dream and put ourselves out there, we're often stopped by doubt and fear. I will show you how to get over those fear barriers so that you do act, demonstrating both the physical and psychological rewards you'll feel if you stick with it and tough it out.

This ICE model is going to be the framework guiding you through your journey of self-discovery, as you discover what it is that inspires you, identify where you can apply more courage, and learn how to face up to fear and act on your goals.

Throughout every chapter, you'll find breakout boxes, encouraging you to reflect on what you want to achieve and what is holding you back. Each exercise and tool in the book will help you unearth your innate potential. The more you put into these exercises, the more you think about them, the more you'll get out. So take your time to understand each one and really think about what I am asking of you.

In each chapter, an 'ICE reflection' box will help you to focus on what you've just learned and realized about yourself.

A bit more about the ICE model

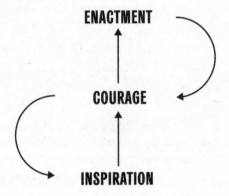

One evening while trying to work out what I would teach to a group of senior leaders at a major car manufacturer the next day – a job I managed to blag in the early days of my coaching career – I stumbled across the ICE model. Looking back over my life and career to that point,

I asked myself how I had achieved so many of the goals I had set myself in life, and then these three words jumped out at me: *Inspiration, Courage, Enactment.*

I scribbled their arrangement down on paper, linking the words together with some arrows, and just like that, the ICE model was born. As I began looking at the details of what I'd written, I realized I'd been following this model my entire life, just without knowing it.

Staring at the three words I realized I might have discovered something extremely simple, but equally profound – a model that can help anyone, at the time when they might be stuck. The following day I delivered it, and from there, the ICE model was embedded within my work.

As simple as traffic lights

When I first devised the ICE model, I was adamant about creating something easy to use and relatable to anyone, while also being highly impactful and effective. I didn't want it to be confusing and overly detailed, so I designed it in a manageable and digestible format applicable to anyone's life, at any age, within any role. Thus, the 'traffic-light' system was born. Red for Inspiration. Amber for Courage. Green for Enactment. You might even grab a few highlighter pens and colour the words accordingly, so that this image sticks in your mind.

Right now, in the ICE model, you're at the beginning point. The red light. Your life may not be working out how you first thought. Alternatively, you may be in a position where you feel you're in a really good place and want to take yourself to the next level. Either way, all you have so far is inspiration. Red is where you stop and remind yourself of why you are doing what you are doing.

As you progress through *Commando Mindset*, you'll see it's all about striving for what you want with precision and clarity. It doesn't mean jumping in with irrationality. It means strategizing, understanding and controlling how you feel, then going straight for what you want. You will need to think with direction and purpose, ultimately deciding to give yourself the green light and take action where others fail.

By the end of the book, you will have a far greater understanding not only of yourself but also of others around you. You will be more confident, courageous, driven, resilient and disciplined.

As a consequence, you'll be far more effective within whatever it is you do.

Whether you're still in school, studying in college or university, working in business, entrepreneurship, sport or any other industry, your potential will be unleashed far more quickly if you learn to live and breathe a Commando mindset.

—Start your Commando mindset journal

In every chapter you'll be asked to reflect on your own life and conduct exercises in the ICE reflection boxes.

For this, I suggest you buy a new notepad (treat yourself to a nice one) and have a pen ready.

On the first page, write COMMANDO MINDSET JOURNAL.

Make it your personal reflection pad. Jot down notes from the exercises, pull out quotes you like, or anything that you think is relevant to your life.

The journal is for your eyes only. It's a safe space where you can write your wildest dreams so keep it close to hand.

Are you ready? Then let's begin.

INSPIRATION

What lies behind you and what lies in front of you,
pales in comparison to what lies inside of you.
Ralph Waldo Emerson

Pinned to the roof

We are deep in the green zone of Afghanistan – a densely vege-tated environment of high crops, trees, fields, ditches and compounds.

For the first time on the tour, our patrol is engaged by the Tali-ban. The enemy directs several bursts of machine-gun fire towards our troop.

For many of us, it's the pop of our cherry, losing our warfare virginity. After months, if not years, of training, we finally experi-ence the deadly realism of combat.

We deal with the contact quickly, before seeking safety within a compound nearby. As a machine gunner, I move to the rooftop on my own, providing cover for my fellow men and women grabbing their breath in the courtyard below.

The roof is completely flat. Zero protection. I feel naked and exposed. The enemy is dangerously close in a battlespace it knows intimately.

Our commander wants to catch the perpetrators who ambushed us so he tasks a team of four guys to move further into the trees. Can they push the insurgents out?

I watch from above as Tats, Al and two more marines move into the treeline and out of sight, stalking our foes.

Out of the corner of my eye, two hundred metres left of where I watched the last man of the team disappear, I notice a lone male peeking around a wall. Watching our every move.

My heart rate increases. The hairs on my neck stand up. Strug-gling to make out anything but his black clothes, I wonder . . .

Am I staring for the first time in my life at an enemy soldier? Is he armed? Or is he a civilian? Has he even seen me?

Deep in the shadow of trees, he's popping his head around the corner of a wall, having a look, then disappearing – a tactic we refer to as 'dicking'.

Nerves pricking, I shout down to Jordan nearby. Telling him what's happening. What can I use for protection?

'Jord, chuck me something up to use as cover.'

My mouth moves, but my eyes are locked on the man's every move.

Only moments ago, the cornfields were alive with rockets, bullets and grenades. The locals are still likely taking cover within the safety of their homes. Yet this guy is out in the open, brashly observing our compound, unperturbed by the violence.

Jordan appears, manhandling a large log he only just manages to shove on the roof. I roll it in front of me and, placing my weapon on top, I sigh with relief. If everything kicks off again, I've got a bit more protection.

Peering around the wall, the man stares directly at me, takes a good look, sinks back into the shadows. In my mind, there's little doubt he's enemy. I'm itching with suspicion, convincing myself there's an AK-47 within arm's length of where he's standing. However, there's little I can do but report down to my commander and keep an eye on him.

Moving my eyes briefly from his position, I check the whereabouts of our four-man team. No sign of them. The thick treeline is obscuring my vision and filling me with unease.

Looking over my shoulder, I start to ask if anyone knows their location. I barely get a few words out before hearing the unmistakable sound of bullets racing over my head.

The firing stops momentarily. Then another burst rattles nearby. And another. Deafening cracks as the rounds whizz inches from me.

I turn my head back, firing a burst from my weapon at the corner of the wall. But the man is gone. The air is silent once more.

This is confusing. I peer over the top of my weapon. Trying to identify the enemy's firing point.

Thump! Crack! Crack! Crack!

Bullets splinter the log in front of me, covering my face with dust and wood chips. My trigger finger reacts. I return bursts of fire into likely enemy areas. Yet I can't identify anything I've been trained to look for. No muzzle flash. No weapon smoke. Nothing.

Crack! Crack! Whizz! Crack! Crack! Crack!

'CONTACT WEST, CONTACT WEST!' I scream down to the others. 'He's fucking got me pinned here!'

Another burst nears me. Frighteningly closer than the last.

The remaining members of the troop jump to their feet and sprint over, calculating what to do next. Yet still out there, all alone, is our small team of four.

Every area I fire into runs the substantial risk of accidentally hitting them, making me pause on every depression of my trigger. I hesitate with every shot, paranoid the team may only be metres from where I lay my fire. The last thing anyone wants is to hit one of your own – a consequence unbearable to live with.

While I'm trapped between my thoughts and actions, the Taliban marksman begins firing at me again. I'm pinned to the roof.

Crack! Whizz! Another few rounds fly over my head. I still can't identify where it's coming from.

I'm questioning my ability to soldier. *Is this guy better than me? Has he got the upper hand? Am I in his sights?*

I can only assume he's shooting through a 'murder hole', squeezing his rifle through a small gap, completely protected from any incoming rounds.

I fire. He answers back. This time with a far longer and more ferocious burst. His rounds are getting closer. Another one ricochets off the log. I stare at it, thankful. *Fuck me! I need to get off this roof.*

By crawling backwards, I'll be able to hit a ledge, reposition myself and return more accurate fire. As I begin moving, more rounds burst over me, forcing me to drag myself quicker. The noise is deafening.

Finally reaching the edge of the roof, I drop my left leg down. It catches on a rusty old hanging basket. The eyelets of my boots are snagging on a loose bit of metal. *A fucking hanging basket will be the reason for my death. Seriously? A fucking hanging basket?*

Again, my adversary's firing intensifies. I'm now contending with ricocheting rounds and a trapped foot. I flash back to that young recruit in the TV ad, submerged within a tunnel on the endurance course.

Panicking, one leg in the air, one hanging down, my head likely within the enemy's sights, I wait for that metal-on-bone thump as the final round strikes me and everything goes dark.

Desperately kicking out, I try to free myself once more.

'FUCK OFF!' I scream. More at the rusty garden feature than the enemy. Then my leg drops down as the hanging basket releases its death grip. Straightaway I take aim and let off a huge burst of machine-gun fire.

'BEN! WAIT!'

Pausing, I recognize the voice, but still take aim again, firing another long and angry burst. Am I losing control?

'OI, BEN! HOLD YOUR FUCKING HORSES. OUR GUYS ARE OUT THERE!'

Looking down, Vicey is staring back up at me, fully in control and unmoved by the situation.

Ducking low, knowing not to leave my head above the ledge as a target, I look down, adrenaline-fuelled, realizing I have possibly overstepped the mark.

'Just wait a minute, hold on,' he says. 'Now, where is the firing coming from?'

Vicey calmly repeats himself with great empathy. He knows exactly how I am feeling. This is a first for me and I've almost been killed in the process. Something my face most definitely reflects.

As Vicey makes his commander's evaluation, I point to where the lone man was once standing.

The Taliban marksman has gone quiet. Dead, or out of ammunition? We'll never know. But he has stopped. And that's enough for me.

Within seconds of the gunfight ending, our four-man team re-enters the compound, with Tats shouting at me, 'You lucky fucker!'

I don't need to hear the rest. I know how lucky I am.

Later that evening, back within the safety of our base, Tats goes into more detail and we reflect on the incident.

From their position, the four-man team couldn't identify the firer. But they could see me, pinned to the roof. Tats describes how rounds were splashing and ricocheting all around me. And that, feeling helpless, all he could do was look on.

INSPIRATION

1.
What Inspirations are and Why They Matter

Our inspirations are sometimes right there staring us in the face:

- *Ever found yourself questioning the reason why you're performing a task?*
- *Has the passion you originally set out with fizzled away?*
- *Feel as if your drive has gone?*
- *Have you simply lost your inspiration?*

Living life to the fullest has become one of my inspirations. I wake up every day committed to ensuring I never rest on my laurels. I continuously pursue excellence and success within whatever it is that I am doing, so that I don't take life and my potential for granted.

What got me here?

During that early operation in Afghanistan, I got stuck in a harsh combat situation for the first time and was convinced my life was over. When a marksman incapacitated my movement, all sorts of woes and regrets whirled around my head. I wished I'd done that extra bit more with my family and friends, and lived my life to the fullest.

There were many more contacts on that day, and during that tour. But, for some reason, that one hit home the most. The feeling of isolation, regret and fear all rolled into one, and I was questioning my own mortality. That very night I vowed to myself that, if I was lucky enough to return home from war, I would live my life as well as I possibly could and without fear or regret. And, if I was going to die so soon, it wouldn't be with my foot stuck in a hanging basket!

I survived and came home.

That experience, early in the tour, sparked an epiphany that life is for living. The feelings it provoked became the inspiration that would propel me forward for years to come.

We are all more capable than we think

I've had my fair share of near-death experiences.

The career I chose meant I was exposed regularly to harm.

On many occasions, I've woken abruptly, in cold sweats, as the fragility of my own mortality set in.

There have been many times when I've seen my life flashing before my eyes. When luck or skill has been all that's kept me alive.

As dangerous as they were, such moments showed me just how much I was taking life for granted.

I saw I was far more capable than I first thought.

Those times proved to me that we are *all* more capable than we think.

Surprisingly, the Taliban marksman taught me an awful lot about myself. I use the inspiration of that experience to overcome trivial matters, doubt, failure and fear; to drive me forward and succeed.

Whether delivering a workshop to senior business leaders, planning another year for my company, helping my children with their homework, washing the car, or just doing the shopping, I keep this inspiration at the forefront of my mind. And connecting with this inspiration is the first step in adopting the Commando mindset.

Commandos
go
that
extra
step
further
and
do
that
little
bit
more
to
succeed.

THAT'S MY INSPIRATION, WHAT'S YOURS?

You needn't have experienced the bloody violence of war, or months of arduous military training, to adopt the Commando mindset.

Nobody in my current organization, apart from my business partner Antony Thompson, has 'commando' in their job title. Yet they are a set of highly driven, motivated, professional and diligent human beings. People who carry out every task with meticulous detail, spurred on by inspirations that incentivize them.

You are like one of these people if you choose to be.

Finding what inspires you will allow you to overcome distractions that might momentarily cloud your judgement and instead put you back on the path to working towards viable and passionate goals.

What inspires people, and how they find that inspiration, differs for everyone. Some may have had an experience early in life that has inspired them to achieve something or work in a certain profession. Other people find their inspiration much later in life.

Whatever your inspiration is or might be, whenever you find it, once you find it you need to keep it at the front of your mind and remind yourself what it is on a daily basis. It's going to get you through thick and thin.

> ## What 'inspiration' means . . .
>
> Dictionary compilers struggle to pinpoint and agree on exactly what an inspiration is. Here are some of the definitions I've found in various dictionaries:
>
> *An inspiring or animating action or influence*
>
> *Something inspired, as an idea*
>
> *A result of inspired activity*
>
> *A thing or person that inspires*
>
> *A divine influence directly and immediately exerted upon the mind or soul*
>
> *The divine quality of the writings or words of a person so influenced*
>
> *The act of inspiring; quality or state of being inspired.*

Whatever you want it to mean

Clearly, an inspiration can be whatever you want it to be. All that matters is that your inspirations have meaning for you.

The title of this chapter promised to reveal what inspirations are. How does that even work if the meaning of the word is so expansive? How do you determine what it is that inspires you? Furthermore, how can your inspirations lead to success?

Thoughts, memories, people, family, work, money, pets, dreams – inspirations can be whatever you choose them to be. Only you will know exactly what they mean to you.

Your inspiration could be the memory of a person who has passed away, as you want to make them proud. It could be completing a physical challenge, like climbing a mountain or running a marathon, or be going after a new job or making your mark in a new industry. You may feel inspired by the need to support your family or be a role model for your children. You might be inspired by the need to save our planet from climate change, or you might be inspired to get in shape so that you can fit into your wedding-day suit or dress!

Inspirations can be fun and make you feel good. An inspiration can make you punch the air with excitement. But it can be a sobering thought too, when you realize how far you have to go.

Whatever they are, inspirations will ignite your enthusiasm and belief.

It's on you

Near the end of this chapter, you'll find your first ICE reflection box, encouraging you to think deeply about what you will carry with you through this book as your inspiration(s).

For now, begin looking around and record in your journal everything that excites and invigorates you. When you get joy out of a certain task write down why it felt good to you. Think about why you did it in the first place and why the reward paid off. Be aware of what is driving you to do the tasks you complete every day. Try to understand what, how and why things may be your inspirations.

> When your alarm goes off in the morning, what is it that stops
> you from pressing 'snooze' and continuing to lie there? What
> drives you to lift your weary head and begin another day?

For many, it is work that propels them out of bed – it brings some financial security and reward, and hopefully, though not always, satisfaction and enjoyment.

For some people, it's being a parent, waking up to remind their children to brush their teeth, ensure milk and cereal aren't spilt all over the kitchen floor, then getting them out of the house in time for the bus.

For others, it's a belief in changing or making a difference for the betterment of society, helping protect their country if working in the military, solving crime if in the police, educating children as a teacher, or raising money and awareness for a charity to help the ill or deprived around the world.

Every morning across the UK, millions of people wake inspired and propelled on by what they do. But many more millions do not.

Which group are you part of, the inspired or the uninspired?

More than this

It isn't just those serving society who start each day driven by the thought of making a difference. The young entrepreneur wakes enthralled by what new opportunities the day could bring. A flourishing executive grasps every chance to watch their company grow stronger. A committed employee wakes up excited to contribute their latest ideas to the projects they care about.

> Wherever you look in the world, there will always be people who are driven by something deeper and more meaningful than just getting by.

For the lucky few, waking in the morning isn't a problem and their vision for the day is clear. Their motivation drives them out of bed, ready to take another step towards making good on their aspirations, dedicated in their pursuit of success. They might be the people you look at begrudgingly, because of how spritely they are on a Monday morning.

At the heart of everything for those types of people is an inspiration. A continuously burning flame of desire that they never allow to die out. Something within them that keeps them going through the hardest of times.

If you don't have an inspiration, it's hard to sit through endless queues of rush-hour traffic, watching the clock tick away like a bomb's countdown timer just to make it into a job you don't like. Squeezing into the last remaining space on the train, packed in like sardines, with your face pressed into a stranger's armpit, you might wonder what it's all for.

Fear not.
You might once have had an inspiration but lost touch with it.
Or maybe you never had one.
But you're going to need it.
In the next few chapters, you'll discover or enhance those you already have.
Then start turning your inspirations into something more than pipe dreams.

Life can be tough, it can be cruel. But it's a lot easier if you have a reason for living it.

The first hurdle in adopting the Commando mindset is to accept this, then work out what it is that's going to propel you over it.

Chuck those rose-tinted glasses away and get ready to work hard.

To obtain success, there must always be sacrifice. Often, this sacrifice is your comfort.

Modern humans who excel do so because they sacrifice comfort for ambition and they value striving for excellence above accepting the average.

YOUR POSITION RIGHT NOW

Hypothetical question. If you had all the money in the world and needn't work again, no more rush-hour queues and armpit-sniffing, what is it that you would set the alarm for? Why would you get out of bed?

Take a moment now to think about the first thing that came to mind and zone in on your gut reaction. What were the first few images or ambitions that leapt into your mind as soon as I extracted the monotony from your life?

Are you left with more motivating and inspiring thoughts?

Are they things you've always wished to achieve or accomplish?

Do they leave you feeling giddy, with a tingling sensation in your stomach?

You will have had a particular reason for picking up this book. Was it simply the title *Commando Mindset* that intrigued you? Was it something in the blurb that caught your attention? Did the idea of achieving something and finding success resonate with you? Did a particular task you face or an adventure you want to go on spring to mind?

What is happening, or not happening, in your life right now that made you pick up this book? Is it a life ambition you seem unable to fulfil?

Whatever the reason, attaining a Commando mindset will help you make good on those ambitions and reach your goals. But you must ask yourself some searching questions.

Why haven't I achieved my ambitions yet?
Why has it taken this book to convince me to take a leap?
If it means so much, why haven't I taken a punt at obtaining what I so desire?
Looking back, have I already tried and failed?
Did I once have an inspiration, but lost it?
What is holding me back?

LIVE LIFE WITHOUT REGRETS

Several years after Afghanistan, I picked up a copy of Stephen R. Covey's *7 Habits of Highly Effective People*, which completely changed my perspective on life.

I had grown a little comfortable again, spending a few months slipping back into an easy routine, not stretching myself. Temporarily, I'd forgotten the adrenaline-filled, near-death experiences and life-changing moments that had driven me; even the Taliban marksman.

Covey poses an intriguing scenario of what your funeral would look like, who would be there, the legacy you left behind and what would be said about you. He then questions your contentment with it. Can you honestly say you're happy with how many people came, who they were and what they said?

It was the hardest-hitting passage in a book I have ever read, yet just what I needed to jump-start my passion for life again, breaking me out of those comfortable and easy routines I'd sunk into. Sometimes, we need a little wake-up call, like this book!

Considering our own mortality often results from learning about other people's near-death experiences, or even their deaths. Being close to death can give anyone a new and profound respect for what's most important in life.

In *The Top Five Regrets of the Dying*, Bronnie Ware, a nurse in palliative care, reveals what the people she cared for entering the last weeks of their lives shared with her before they passed. So that we don't make the same mistakes and take similar regrets to our graves, the author highlights key areas we all overlook. Bronnie discovered five profound observations and a distinct commonality within all regrets:

- *I wish I'd had the courage to live a life true to myself, not the life others expected of me.*
- *I wish I hadn't worked so hard.*
- *I wish I'd had the courage to express my feelings.*
- *I wish I had stayed in touch with my friends.*
- *I wish I had let myself be happier.*

You can't help but pause and consider these regrets. I'm imagining that at least one of them is true for you now. We end up regretting simple day-to-day actions, where we feel we could have done a little more, or something different.

Many of us carry such thoughts that burden us for years, ignoring and suppressing them in order to get by, make ends meet, or keep other people happy. Thoughts that possibly we too will lie with upon our deathbeds and repeat to carers like Bronnie.

So, why do we let it get to such a point?

Why is it only the people who recover from serious illness or injury, or narrowly escape deadly situations – the *survivors* – who get smacked with the wake-up call?

Why did getting pinned to a roof by a Taliban marksman become my wake-up call?

If you're reading this then you're alive (obviously) and, more importantly, have the opportunity to make a change. You can do something about it and turn the *I wish* into *I should* or, better yet, *I can* and *I will*.

I will have the courage to live a true life, not the life others expected of me. I will let myself be happier.

Awe-inspiring

We don't always have to contemplate death or be facing an almost near-death experience in order to change our lives. We can find inspiration through a different kind of reflection. One that looks to our awe-inspiring surroundings.

Think about the tiny blue-and-green marble we call home. We float through the abyss of space, a universe packed full of trillions of stars, galaxies, planets, rocks and ice, moving at unimaginable speeds, narrowly avoiding existential dangers we can't see. We're lucky in every sense to be living on this planet.

And are we not also just as fortunate to be the result of the right sperm meeting with the right egg to form our impressive lives? Within a time so generously rich in opportunity and freedom? On what seems like the only life-sustaining planet within trillions of miles?

Have we not been gifted an unbelievable opportunity to make something of ourselves? The chance to make the most of what equates to a blink of an eye in space-time? To do something completely different from the daily grind?

Just why would we allow ourselves to keep falling into a moaning, groaning, monotonous existence, finally lying upon our deathbeds accompanied by nothing but regret?

Why would *you*?

Thinking about this question will help you work out your unique inspiration in life.

When you have an idea about what you're inspired by, write it down in your journal.

It doesn't have to be one thing, it can be three, five, or even ten things. All that matters are that these thoughts and ideas inspire *you*.

As you progress through this book, it will become very clear why having meaningful inspirations is very important. Having inspirations will pull you out of destructive behaviours or comfortable habits and springboard you out of bed each day. Your inspirations will be the foundations of your success, driving you on when you fall on adverse and difficult times.

ICE reflection 1:
Initial inspirations

Your first ICE reflection is a simple one, but I warn you, it may draw out a few unwanted memories.

I want you to think about what Bronnie Ware found with those who spent their final days in her care and relate them to your own regrets. Everyone carries a degree of regret, so feel no shame in those you have, big or small. We hear it preached regularly that everyone should try harder to live without regret. But just how feasible is that?

Consider the following questions and write down your answers in your journal. The information you put is for your eyes only, so be as detailed as you want – there's no judgement here.

What are your three biggest regrets?

For each regret, can you find two reasons why you have it?

Do your inspirations in any way relate to your regrets?

A point of clarity: the reason I want you to point out any regrets to yourself is not so that you can put any of them right.

Instead, it's important that the inspirations you choose are ones that will work for you and your future success. I'm simply asking you to learn from what has passed, to find the positives and opportunities for growth and be ready to embrace new challenges.

The next chapter will focus on helping you find your inspiration and bring it to life. In it, we'll unearth some of your inspirations that we can later transform into goals.

Anyone can change

Wednesday morning. My bedroom, Mum's house.

Blocked nose, stuffed eyes, aching jaw. My head feels like it's clamped in a vice. Teeth locked together, chewing on nothingness.

I am numb. Emotionally broken, beyond crying and sorrow. All down to the sinister white powder. Staring out through half-pulled blinds, the outside world trying to peep between each gap into the dark room.

Is this what despair feels like?

Clothes strewn across the floor. Dirty laundry, dirty plates, magazines and rubbish littering my bedroom, reflecting the chaos and disorder of my mind and life. My jaw clenches even tighter as I cast my eyes upon the mess. I let out a long sigh of shame.

Where, how and when will I do it?

Do I even have the ability to do the unthinkable?

Should I take an overdose, use a noose, jump off something?

My thoughts are dark, the darkest they've ever been, but deep within, part of me is trying to break out and scream. It doesn't quite make it and I remain silent, accepting my bleak fate.

I take the CD case with two more lines of cocaine – evil white trails of addiction. I curse the drug before inhaling another hit through a rolled-up receipt.

My heart rate spikes. For a moment, I felt free again. Wired and ready. The unmistakable sensations coke induces.

But it isn't long before the euphoric feelings wear off and I'm craving another snort. Cocaine. It hits you, addicts you, leaves you wanting more. Then it sprints away with your freedom and ambitions.

My cruel paranoia and dark thoughts quickly return, ruining my short-lived fun.

Fuck it, I want out!

Here I am, unemployed, depressed, addicted to one of the world's most dangerous drugs. Sniffing away on my own in my mum's spare bedroom, as my family and friends work hard away on their careers.

That's it, I've had enough . . .

Seconds, minutes, or possibly hours later I'm slumped on a chair staring at the bright computer screen; YouTube videos stare back at me. I've bottled it. I couldn't go through with the unthinkable. Well, not today, anyway. Maybe I'll bring myself to do it tomorrow.

In a haze of laziness, I click on an old Royal Marines commercial. Then I see the advert.

99.99% need not apply.

I get up and return to my room. Something has clicked in my head, but I can't tell what.

Did that call to action just save my life?

I can't stop thinking about that ad. The marine's rifle and camouflage, the speedboat at the end. And, of course, that infamous green beret.

Battling the muddy assault course to join the elite, that Royal Marines recruit is a far cry from the wreck in the mirror. Upstairs, sitting on my bed again, half of me envies the young man as he strives for his own green beret.

Was he once like me?

Did he also have to change?

Is it a sign? Did that advert find me?

Was it a coincidence?

Finally, something clicks in my mind.

The thirty-second ad carries me back fifteen years. I am suddenly a five-year-old boy, standing in the Royal Marines museum, assessing every picture and story in detail. My childish self is in utter awe of the men portrayed wherever he turns. He dreams of one day becoming a Commando.

The TV advert has reminded me of my childhood ambition, something I had not thought about for years.

While growing up, a career in the military had always been my goal, but somewhere along the path I took some very wrong turnings. I had lost myself to violence, drugs and alcohol and it had ruined me. I realize I've been trying to live as someone else; a tough guy craving the hard life. But look where it's led me – broke, depressed, in debt and unemployable.

For the first time in many years, something refreshing dawns on me. At last, I realize who I could be – an adult version of that giddy child in the museum.

Up until now, all that has inspired me is finding the next high that will smother my depressive feelings – using the blanket of drugs to hide from the pain of existence. But now, something new looms on the horizon. I feel that, deep down, I am meant to be a Royal Marines Commando. And who knows what else I could be.

Have I finally discovered a new inspiration?

I find myself picking up the magazines strewn across my floor. I collect the many days' worth of dirty plates and glasses, taking them downstairs to wash up. I separate my clean and unwashed clothes, folding everything away into my drawers, stuffing laundry into the washing machine. I dust my shelves and straighten up pictures and ornaments. I change my bed and open the windows.

I am trying to discipline myself like a soldier. It feels good. It feels refreshing.

I am fucking taking the control back.

The following morning, with my room tidy, I plough through the downstairs cupboard where everyone hoards their shoes. *There must be some in here that still fit me.* I pluck out a pair of well-worn trainers. They will have to do.

Searching through the airing cupboard, I find a mismatched T-shirt and tracksuit bottoms and quickly put them on.

'Keep going, Ben,' I say out loud to myself. 'Keep changing.'

Standing at my front door, dressed like someone kitted out from a school's lost property bin, I breathe in the fresh air.

I haven't sniffed or smoked drugs in over twenty-four hours. Even that is enough time to feel the difference. My suicidal thoughts have scared me away from the poison. For now. But I must stay in control.

The day is cool, and a low mist fills the air licking at my skin. I feel invigorated, seeing the world differently than I did just a day or two ago.

Is this what it's like, daring to change?

Taking one step, then another, I begin jogging down my road. My legs hurt and my body creaks. My lungs are desperately telling me to stop. But my mind is now intoxicated with some new sensation, the feeling of drive and success – I am clawing back purpose.

There is no going back now, this is the new me. Tonight, I will tell my girlfriend and family that I am going to sign up to the Royal Marines.

2.
Find Your Inspiration and Accept It Might Change

BE FLEXIBLE FOR CHANGE

As you build on the last chapter and you begin to think about narrowing down your inspirations, it's important to remember that, along your journey, your inspirations will change, deviate and evolve. Some may stick with you for a lifetime and others may disappear as you tick them off your list. This is natural. Different inspirations will see you through varied experiences.

In the build-up to Commando training, my inspiration was to get clean from drugs and become fit, before getting accepted onto the thirty-two-week course. Then, as I progressed through training, my inspiration became earning the famous green beret.

When I deployed to Afghanistan, my inspiration evolved into keeping my friends safe so that we could all go home alive. And I knew that when I returned home, because of that fateful episode on the roof of that compound where my life flashed before my eyes, I would be inspired to live life to the fullest.

When I formed my first business, my inspiration was to ensure

I built a business model that would become profitable within two years, then support and sustain further business concepts.

When I married and became a father, my family became my biggest inspiration. Now, everything I do is for them – an inspiration that will likely stay at the top of my list for ever.

Like I said, inspirations come and go, change or stay. Getting through training was a short-term inspiration, but my family will forever be my lifetime inspiration.

— Pause for thought —

Reflect on some of the inspirations that you may have felt in your life. Can you spot short-term or long-term inspirations from your past?

Do you recognize inspirations that were deep-rooted?

How about others that were flexible and changed?

Can you identify inspirations that once drove you but now no longer exist?

What are your inspirations that have stood the test of time?

Briefly homing in on the inspirations that have changed, ask yourself why they changed.

Did you quit on it very early?

Did you pursue something that deeply inspired you for a long time but then gave up on it at the last hurdle?

Was your inspiration short lived because you found a new inspiration?

Did you simply forget about your inspiration while going through the daily grind of life?

Think about your long-standing inspirations.

How come they've made it to this point while the others haven't?

Through reflecting on these answers, try to recognize what drives you and what does not.

EVOLVE YES, QUIT NEVER

Change is inevitable. Your life will naturally steer you away or distract you from certain inspirations and sometimes pull you towards new ones. I encourage you to allow this to happen as organically as possible as this can keep your life fun and fresh. When you no longer feel inspired to keep striving, when your flair and passion for something have naturally died out, that's OK. You are allowed to be flexible and adapt to your circumstances, coming up with new inspirations when appropriate.

But there's a fine balance between allowing your inspirations to be flexible and repeatedly changing them but never following through. The boxed reflection exercise on pages 55–6 should help you understand why and how you have been inspired by different things over the course of your life so far.

If something inspires you, it will feel as if it is coming from deep within and will form the basis of your goals. My family is my inspiration, so I can base my goals around that, ensuring I can provide the best life for them:

Inspiration	Goals
My Family	Work hard and earn more money for them.
	Take more holidays.
	Set more time aside for family time in day-to-day life.
	Help with my children's homework three times a week.

These specific goals may change along the way – as my children get older and I no longer have to help them with homework, say – but the inspiration always remains my family. This is my driver, and this helps me focus on what I'm doing and stay on course. Later, I'll ask you to think about your own inspirations and goals and list them in your journal.

When people fail to complete their goals it is usually because they have lost their burning, inspiration-driven desire to achieve them. If you're no longer inspired by what you are doing, and why you are doing it, then it is highly likely you won't reach any associated goals.

You must be tenacious. You have to own an unflinching desire to do the tasks you set yourself.

> Either succeed in what you're doing, or exhaust every possible avenue before you decide to change the plan. Otherwise you'll never achieve anything.

Is it boring to keep plugging away at an inspiration, continually trying and failing? Yes, some of your journey will be monotonous and tough and disheartening. Not every meeting will feel charged. Not every run will be enjoyable. Not every lesson will keep you wired. Michael Phelps, Oprah Winfrey, Bill Gates, Mark Zuckerberg, Serena Williams, J. K. Rowling and many other figures the world admires all had to keep going when quitting seemed the only option. Don't give up on your inspirations. Try hard enough and you will eventually succeed.

GET PASSIONATE

In his book *The Psychology of Passion*, psychologist Robert J. Vallerand observes that feeling a harmonious passion for a task can greatly improve your performance, meaning it becomes part of your identity.

You want to feel engaged by what inspires you, especially when transforming your inspirations into goals.

The message I will continuously drive home throughout this book is just as simple . . .

> Your inspirations *need* to light a fire in your belly every time you think of them.

If your inspirations are truly aligned to what you *really* want to achieve – and you're passionate about them – finding the motivation to achieve them shouldn't be difficult. You will often find yourself in a state of 'flow' when immersed in the doing of a task associated with your inspirations. This is a clear sign that what you have picked to succeed at is right for you.

Flow

Ever been sat doing a task where you missed lunch without knowing, day has faded to night, what seemed like minutes was in fact hours?

First coined by Hungarian-American psychologist Mihály Csíkszentmihályi, 'flow' has become more widely known as 'being in the zone'.

It refers to when a person performing an activity owns a feeling of energized focus and enjoyment in the task. Becoming deeply immersed in what they are doing. So fully involved that their sense of time and space is lost. They're absorbed in the moment.

ENJOY IT IF YOU CAN

For a journey to be worthwhile, you need to be able to enjoy the doing of a task just as much as you would enjoy the satisfaction of completing it.

This doesn't necessarily mean that every task you undertake needs to be done with a big smile on your face and continuous enthusiasm. Many challenges that lie ahead will be fraught with difficulty and cause unease – this is part of the process. But you have to be able to allow yourself to feel achievement and joy in the small stuff along the way.

Enjoyment stems from knowing you are moving towards the completion of your goals. That everything you undertake – difficult or easy – is for a reason and part of your progress.

Monotonous tasks are part of our lives and must be expected, but I want you to find satisfaction in the small steps that will lead you to achieve your dreams. Remembering why you are doing the small task, and tapping back into your inspiration, will help you enjoy the process and keep driving you forward.

Before you progress into the next chapter, work through ICE reflection 2. Identify the inspirations that drive you and that you are going to take with you through this book. Use this exercise to understand what it is you want to achieve and why, as well as establishing the relation between your inspirations and your values.

ICE reflection 2:
Discovering your inspirations

Think deeply about the questions below and identify how you feel when you answer each one.

Remember, to form actionable goals from your inspirations, they MUST mean something to you.

After each question, I've added some suggested answers to help get you thinking about what your inspirations might be. But remember, they are just that – *your* inspirations. And they can be anything you want them to be.

What makes you feel happy? *You may write your children, partner, work or business, fitness, finances, or education as what makes you feel happy and inspires you.*

Which of these can be made into a tangible goal? *You then need to turn one of your inspirations into a tangible goal like:*

Children → provide financially for your children and/or raise healthy and happy children.

Partner → have a fulfilling relationship with your partner; go on a date night once a month.

Work/business → create a business plan or strategy to set up your new company or work towards a promotion.

Sport → learn how to play a new sport or join a gym or find a personal trainer in order to get fit.

Finances → make a personal savings plan or look for new ways to invest your money.

Education → take a new course or sign up to teach a skill you have to other people.

You might have many different inspirations, all of the above and more, perhaps. That's OK. If you want to work out goals for every one of your inspirations then you can, but I'd encourage you not to focus on too many at any one time because it's difficult to balance a lot of different goals. If you have several inspirations, pick three to focus on now. It doesn't mean the others aren't important, it's just that you're prioritizing some that are more important to you at present. Once you've worked through the book with a few dreams and goals, you can always come back to it again with other goals in mind.

OK, so now it's time for you to write down your inspirations in your journal and the corresponding goals.

Once you've done that, sign and date your list and get ready to move on to making these dreams a reality.

INSPIRATIONS AND GOALS

What I love most about an inspiration – and what will become apparent as you progress through this book – is that, no matter how tough your journey gets or how great is the adversity you meet, your inspirations will always be there for you, acting as your reminder and encouragement to keep going.

There have been countless times when I questioned myself – as have you, I'm sure – whether it was when I was waist deep in a bog on Dartmoor at midnight, pinned to the roof by the Taliban marksman, competing for business in a difficult market, or becoming a dad for the first time.

No matter how dark or daunting the moment may feel, taking a second to remind yourself of your inspiration can help you through. Just a tiny switch of thought can remind you why you have committed to such a task and allow the clarity and encouragement you need to kick back in.

You must find a way to remind yourself of your ambitions on a daily basis. There are many ways to do this, one of which is to provide yourself with an inspiration reminder in the form of a visual aid. It's a method I use myself.

Inspiration reminder: Make yourself a 'cue card'

Even if you are deeply driven by an inspiration, you will still have days when you must remind yourself why you are doing what you are doing. That could be when adversity strikes, difficulty sets in, or motivation is lacking.

Have to hand a simple aid that will reignite your drive. If your family are your inspiration, keep a small laminated picture of them with you at all times. When you're digging deep, or needing that inspiration when working on a goal, pull it out, look at it and remind yourself of what it is that inspires you: *your family.*

You can find a visual aid for any inspiration, whether it's to live a life of adventure and travel the world, amass more money, achieve a certain body shape or weight, or quit your job and work for yourself.

Commando values

Shovelling in one last bite. Washing it down with bottled water, hot from the sun. Taste buds numb to the monotonous flavour of rations. Then the distant sound of an explosion, followed by gunfire, stops my chewing dead.

'Get your kit on, lads. Be at the north gate in five!' the boss calls out.

Sharing the small base with our thirty-strong troop are twelve Scots Guards from the British army. They have just walked straight into a Taliban ambush.

With no time for questions or updates, I grab my stuff and race to the north gate.

Whenever a patrol goes out on the ground – protecting the area outside the base – another group of soldiers designated as a QRF (quick reaction force) waits inside, ready to move out at a moment's notice if the patrol comes under attack.

When you're part of a QRF you sit by your kit and weapon, poised and ready in case another call sign needs assistance.

'Right, the Scots are pinned down only four hundred metres west from us,' explains the boss. 'Plan is, head out in our normal order of march fast, reach the northern area of this field and divert the enemy's attention,' he continues.

As the boss rattles off his set of orders, I nod along in agreement, listening intently.

'Lads,' he says, 'mortars are going to fire us in to make our approach safer. Keep your heads low for any frag and be wary of where things are dropping.'

Our mortar fire controller (MFC) is going to coordinate the bombs that will land in front of us as we approach the position, slowly progressing with us and acting as a curtain of protection.

'It will be close, lads, so keep an eye out,' the MFC adds.

It's organized chaos as everyone dives about on autopilot,

readying themselves for another scrap with the enemy. Sharply pulling on my gun's cocking handle, I make my weapon ready to fire and check my kit.

Overhearing frantic radio messages coming in from the pinned Scots and two-way gunfire in the direction of the ambush, we all suddenly find that extra bit of speed in getting ready.

'When you're set, lads, move out.' The boss gives us the thumbs up and we are out of the gate.

Our pace is unusually quick, considering the high density of IEDs in the area. It's not how we would normally patrol as we'd usually take our time to minimize the risk of getting blown up, but there's no room for caution right now. We have to be quick and get to the ambush before any serious injuries – or, worse, deaths – occur.

'*Inbound!*' screams a voice from the back of the patrol.

An almighty explosion. A few hundred metres in front of us. An eruption of dust and dirt, debris and vegetation violently disturbs the air, producing a plume of thick black smoke and fire. Our first protective mortar has landed. Several more swiftly follow. Earth-shuddering explosions detonate dangerously close.

'Go firm,' the boss's voice halts us in our tracks. 'Let them drop,' he commands. And we watch the landscape before us disintegrate in immense mushroom clouds of hot fragmentation and mud.

A final mortar explodes. We push on. 'Best speed, lads,' the boss encourages.

This mission is important. Yet at any moment we might trigger an IED. I'm just waiting for my world to explode as I watch my legs leave my body and fly through the air.

We're moving so quickly it's impossible to check for any signs of booby traps or IEDs. But we crack on, regardless. This isn't a moment for caution or doubt, but instead for excellence and self-discipline, battling out any intrusive thoughts.

Unmistakably near to our south-west, gunfire from the Scots is getting louder, as they battle with a fierce enemy.

'Do they know we're here, boss?' my corporal, Zach, calls out.

'Yep,' comes the reply. 'I've radioed through. They've got eyes on us now.'

'More rounds incoming!' yells the MFC, ordering us to get low. 'These ones will be much closer.' He isn't wrong.

Huge explosions boom, deafening us all as they land close by, a dangerous hundred metres to our front. Concussive noise rocks my entire body with brutal blows.

Feeling like Tom Hanks in *Saving Private Ryan*, I hesitantly peek up at the mortar's huge plume, debris and rocks raining on us all. Each explosion creates frightening shards of red-hot shrapnel that pass only metres overhead.

A final round explodes. The smoke and dust leave a wall of cover, concealing our approach.

Ready for our final dash, the boss coordinates with the Scots to up their rate of fire. This gives us further cover, distracting the Taliban while we make our dangerous move onto the position.

'*Fucking go, lads! Move! Move! Move!*' shouts the boss, as we quickly scramble to our feet and begin a gut-busting sprint.

Burning and fatiguing, my quad muscles seem to be moving my legs at a snail's pace.

Diving to the floor and out of breath, with the metallic taste of blood and lactic acid in my dust-dry mouth, I place my weapon in my shoulder and begin firing down an alleyway.

Damo and Dave join me. We hammer the area from which the enemy ambushed the Scots. As more of our troop enter the fight, together we're executing controlled yet extreme violence. Bringing an overwhelming weight of concentrated firepower onto the unsuspecting Taliban position.

There's no reply from our enemy. As we pour our ammunition into where they are, we won't let them reply.

'Keep it up, lads, you're smashing them!' Our boss is receiving updates from the Scots' commander, who can see where our rounds are landing, reporting that those who haven't been shot are fleeing.

Overhead, two roaring USMC AH-1 Super Cobras join in the fight. Attack helicopters circle above like preying hawks.

An air of confidence sweeps over us all. Throughout the tour, we have forever been on the back foot, losing so many good guys and girls to the Taliban's deadly guerrilla warfare. But today, we are in control.

For the first time, we have the upper hand. The enemy is cornered. Many of them are seeing out the last few minutes of their lives.

Yet this is when our Commando values kick in most. We are not bloodthirsty animals, but trained marines who uphold what we stand for in any situation. And we have a job to do that's nearing completion.

We are here to bail out the army regiment.

Now that we are in control, the Scots are making a quick dash back to the base, their ammunition almost gone. We finish off the fight with our enemy.

As the Cobras radio through that they are 'Winchestered' – a term meaning all ammunition expended – we begin our own withdrawal.

Patrolling back. The air suddenly still, screened in dust, smoke and the distant muffled thump of Cobra rotor blades. I reflect on what we've just done. We saved the day.

As we enter the base, there's every opportunity for the infamous marines vs army banter. Yet, for some reason today, we hold back on our sarcasm and humour. Both are kept in check by our values.

The Scots' patrol commander comes over, shaking our hands and thanking us, swiftly followed by his men. Their gratitude is clear.

Before today's ambush, we've bonded little with the Scottish troop. They have their part of the base and we have ours. No integration. The Scots are completely detached from their own unit, embedded in the heart of Taliban territory with a bunch of marines.

From today, it all changes. An immense amount of respect is formed. We become a larger brotherhood, no matter the cap badge. For me, this day is one of the clearest examples of Commando values in action.

Excellence: strive to do better.

Integrity: tell the truth.

Self-discipline: resist the easy option.

But there is another founding Commando value:

Humility: respect the rights, diversity and values of others.

It's humility that allows us to forge these new relationships with the Scots. I respect everything they're doing for us. Relieving some of the burden we face. Without them, we'd be on our arses. I admire this. We all do.

Every man in my troop would risk his life again and again for them if it came to it – all thanks to our Commando values.

From now on, while the Scots continue to assist us at the base, we'll train together in the day and share stories around fires at night. We'll do our jobs together, patrolling the battlefields and securing the base.

INSPIRATION

3.
Make Your Values the Difference Between Winning and Losing

USE WHAT YOU VALUE TO PUSH YOURSELF FURTHER

When I'm delivering talks and workshops, one particular question nearly always arises: *Why are Royal Marines Commandos deemed elite?* It's a question I love responding to, as the answer is so simple. Because of our values.

It's not just physical actions in battle that make Royal Marines Commandos who we are, nor the months of arduous training and exercises. Consider recent military history, a timeline engulfed with conflicts in Iraq and Afghanistan. Hundreds of thousands of British troops have fought together and worked side by side for years on end. Yet, for some reason, the Royal Marines gain a higher sense of recognition.

As members from across all three armed forces – the RAF, the Royal Navy and the British army – have committed to an equally commendable effort, recognition should not go solely to the Royal Marines. But, when people are asked to name elite military outfits, along with the special forces and the Parachute Regiment, the Royal Marines stand out clearly at the top. And it is because of the values embedded in our culture.

I believe that having strong personal values goes a long way in carrying you to success. Having values can help bridge the gap from inspiration to courage. Your strong personal values will give you the courage to action your goals and accelerate you towards your dream.

> The standout attribute that, in the eyes of the world, places the Royal Marines Commandos above the rest is our elite way of thinking that is centred around the values we live and die by.

Quickly flick back through your notes from ICE reflection 2 and cast your eyes over the inspirations you wrote down.

Remember, they needed to make you feel excited and driven, and be relevant to what you *truly* want to achieve in life. Deep somewhere within those inspirations are your values, key principles you want to live your life by. Keep your inspirations in mind as you work through this chapter.

VALUES ARE TRANSFORMATIVE

Before I joined the marines, I thought I never owned any values. Yet I clearly valued getting high!

When I joined the Commandos, however, I was given a set of values that every marine lived and breathed – values that will stay with me for the rest of my life.

I found it fascinating to see that when people who joined up with or after me, and who had also previously owned very few values, were literally *issued* some values, they transformed into characters of the utmost discipline and excellence, becoming some of the world's toughest and most professional soldiers.

If you don't recognize your values yet, the next part of this book will help you discover a useful and meaningful set of values to live by.

If you do own a set of values you consciously live by, I want you to think hard about how seriously you are taking them, questioning whether they are right for you, and how often you make decisions that conform to them or even think about them.

From now on, your values need to be clearly aligned to your inspirations and goals while reflecting your personality and what you stand for. *Make your values only about you.* If you do, your chances of success are far greater.

I have designed a quick-fire test to help you work out what those values might be. From the list of values, pick out some words that you are drawn to. This list is only a starting point, it's not exhaustive. You might have a value in mind that isn't even on it – if so, that's great!

—Quick-fire test—

In your journal, write down the values that call out to you in the following list:

Integrity	Security	Curiosity
Excellence	Happiness	Belonging
Service	Friendship	Freedom
Growth	Community	Loyalty
Quality	Challenge	Stability
Family	Empathy	Exploration
Innovation	Accountability	Adventure
Faith	Money	Choice
Health	Success	Control
Fitness	Vision	Justice
Discipline	Humility	Modesty
Love	Wellness	Respect
Leadership	Education	Honour
Strength	Learning	Drive

Then think about and write down the answers to the following questions:

What do these values mean to you?
What made you choose them?
Do you believe in them?

This exercise is the first step to working out your values. Further exercises will build on this and you might end up choosing some of these words as your values or coming up with entirely new ones.

For now, I want you to ask yourself and answer honestly, *Do you live by the values you wrote down now?*

LIVING WITH AND BY YOUR PERSONAL VALUES

The last question in the quick-fire test is the most important one. Do you live by your personal values? It's one of the first questions I always ask any person or organization I consult or coach with. Sadly, I am greeted so often with the same embarrassed answers. 'No, not really.' And that's if people can tell me what their personal values are in the first place.

Be honest with yourself – did you find it easy to think about your values, or did you struggle, feeling as if you were clutching at straws just to get something written down?

Through my business, I have worked with so many people who lack clarity in what they believe in and value, who consequently stumble through life and work with no real clear vision. People who, when asked what their values are, simply shrug – exactly what I would have done if you'd asked me before I joined the Commandos.

Happily, I've also encountered hundreds, if not thousands, of people who believe in and rigorously follow their values. And these are usually the most successful people who, perhaps unsurprisingly, put their good fortune down to sticking with what they believe in.

How do you know if you live by your values?

I'd like you to think about an occasion on which you have committed to and succeeded at something that really excited you.

Were the reasons for your success based upon what you stood for at the time?
Did you commit because something in you said it was right for you or what you were meant to do?
If yes, what do you think drove this way of thinking? Was it your internal values?

Now consider the tasks you didn't succeed at.

What broke down during the journey that caused the aspiration not to come to fruition?
Can you identify any correlations between what you succeeded at and what you didn't?
Was there something missing that hindered you in pursuing what you thought you desired?
Do you think your personal values, or lack of them, had anything to do with these outcomes?

VALUES AT WORK

It's not just personal values that are important; your company or work-place values matter too. I work with organizations that are often struggling, wanting to improve, or looking for a fix.

'No one seems to care about the company values,' is a complaint I hear all the time from the CEOs of major corporations.

It's not surprising that those corporations struggle to get their people to buy into their own organizational values, because in nearly every case that set of values is not *meaningful*.

Their values focus on customers and not employees. They lack definition and feel general, or as though they could belong to any other company in their industry. They aren't tailored to that specific company and their workforce. These grand-sounding values are well meaning but they don't feel accessible or individual, and, as such, staff just simply can't get behind them or embody them.

Often, it's the company's very values that are letting the organization down. Because they're not the *right values*.

Now, I want you to think less about your personal values and more about your organization's . . . If your company or place of work is run according to a set of values, do you commit to them? Do your colleagues know and understand them? A typical set might look something like this:

- Direct, truthful and open communication
- Commitment to clients and customers
- Honesty in the workplace
- Innovation
- Fairness
- Collaboration
- Leadership
- Respect
- Dedication

At work, do you find yourself surrounded by such words?

Does your business state that you should believe in, buy into and/or act out these values?

How do these values make you feel?

Are they worth your time and effort to adopt?

TYING YOUR VALUES TO YOUR WORK

The Royal Marines' values stem from the men who set them many years ago and are the words of our military ancestors. When recruits join training, they are required to learn the values their predecessors set, continuing to uphold what has always been there.

More importantly, however, our values carry real meaning and are inextricably connected to the work we do. They are there to support the organization, in foundations that have stood the test of time. However, these organizational values possess such meaning that *every* marine embodies and lives by them, embracing them as his or her own personal values.

Are your company values this strong? Do you believe in them? Do you live by them outside the office too? If your company doesn't have a set of values, could you suggest some to senior management? If you are senior management, or if you are a business owner, one of the best things you can do for your company and staff is to instil a strong sense of values. So, what are you waiting for?

WHAT SECRET FORMULA?

In November 2018, my business partner Antony and I were invited to Cheltenham Town FC to help improve the team's performance with our Finding Your Edge workshop – a favourite of ours.

Former Burnley defender Michael Duff looked as if his managerial career was about to suffer a very early plummet, not long after taking over the reins of a failing club. Duffy expressed concern to us over the fact the team wasn't gelling. If they didn't commit to something drastically different they were destined for relegation from League Two, and he himself would be heading for a sacking.

The Robins' performance had been shocking, with a measly eight points on the board from sixteen games. Sitting third from bottom of the lowest division, having won only one game, they faced an unenviable drop into non-league football. With only half a day to make a difference, Antony and I faced our own greatest challenge in business until that point.

Personal and organizational values play a huge part in the Finding Your Edge workshop, but I'd be lying if I said I thought values were the root of the team's problems.

However, an hour into the session, it was evident that Cheltenham Town didn't own a single value as a club – *not one!* The players had their own personal values, but the club had none. On making that surprising discovery, we gathered together everyone connected with the club and encouraged them to come up with four values that they could all commit to. Then we had those values printed and displayed throughout the training facility and stadium – values the team had collectively established and, more importantly, believed in.

Cheltenham went on to win twenty of their remaining thirty league games that season, drawing seven and losing only three. Had they performed all year as they did from the day we visited, they would have probably won promotion, if not the league.

When Alan Smith – senior football writer at *The Times* – rang to ask how the hell we'd had such an immediate and profound impact on the struggling team, I was dubious about revealing our methods. As he probed further, Smith referenced how Duff had attributed the team's success to our work with them, which humbled me greatly.

That said, there was no secret formula, merely an observation we made and suggested to everyone. I told Smith we'd advised the club, not just the players – including everyone from chairman and directors through to the tea lady and kit man – that they should agree on a set of values that every player could believe in and live by, on and off the pitch.

Though the article published in *The Times* was headlined 'The Former Marines Who Have Become Football's Repair Men', all we did was point out the obvious.

It was the same when we coached MBE and Olympian Casey Stoney's Manchester United Ladies. Establishing collectively agreed, meaningful values was a major progress point when I worked with the England football team and several other high-profile professional sporting outfits.

Of course, the Finding Your Edge workshop isn't applicable only to football. We've also implemented it in the financial and banking industry, commerce, construction and the automotive industry with amazing results. The key is to establish a set of meaningful and believable values both personally and organizationally, then witness the change.

With every organization I have worked alongside, I continuously state the same observation made to me when I was a young recruit: 'This is not a job, it's a lifestyle.'

So you're clear – if you are to develop a similar Commando mindset, you too must formulate a set of personal values and take them seriously. Day and night, at home and at work. That is the only option.

—Pause for thought—

Near the end of this chapter, you'll have the opportunity in ICE reflection 3 to determine or even establish a set of personal values you can live by. However, spend a few minutes now thinking about what you have read. As your understanding of values and their importance is growing, can you now identify moments and areas in your life where your personal values are more evident than you first thought? You needn't write them down, just bear them in mind for the next part of this chapter.

VALUES VS FEELINGS

We live in a society driven by feelings, where many of our actions are generated by our short-term desires.

While feelings are very important in the correct context, people seem far too quick these days to drop their pen, put away their trainers, have that drink they promised themselves they wouldn't have, close that book and turn on the TV, or choose cheesy fries over a salad.

Many of us live for the moment, satisfying current desires that make us feel good in the now, but not necessarily in the long run. Of course, a certain amount of this is OK, but if we always act on our in-the-moment feelings rather than with our long-term goals in mind, we stop ourselves from progressing.

How many of your decisions are determined by how you are feeling at a particular moment, dictated by irrational thoughts and behaviours?

You must not see feelings as a hindrance. Of course, they are extremely important to your decision making. Without feelings, you would be numb and emotionless, not the nicest type of person to be around; but consider on how many occasions you make a decision based on what you feel at the time.

Ideally, your decisions should be made with integrity, based upon your values, decided upon with logic and clarity, aligning with what is most important to you in life.

VALUES	FEELINGS
principles or standards of behaviour	emotional states or reactions
Do you work hard at sticking to your goals, remaining focused on the long run and ignoring those annoying irrational behaviours?	Do you lack fulfilment because you get distracted by easy options? Does the immediate seem more appealing than the delayed?

You will never be able to take full and positive actions that can turn your dreams into reality if you constantly follow your feelings. If you follow your feelings, you will be susceptible to distraction and take the easy option, and therefore your mission will not succeed.

Be honest with yourself and think about how you make decisions. Are you guided by your values or your feelings?

Never take it easy

I remember my corporal in training pointing to a huge hill, with deep and steep re-entrants – a cutting in the high feature, eroded over thousands of years by running water.

The cuttings made for an extremely demanding ascent, one that would likely test the strongest of men. To the west of the cuttings sat an even slope that provided an easy and gradual approach to the summit.

'Which way are we going, Williams?'

'West, Corporal – the most energy efficient route.'

'Wrong. The enemy will be focused on the west because of its easy approach. We will take the hardest and most difficult route possible, because they won't be expecting it. Life isn't about taking the easy option, it's about enduring challenge that benefits the long run.'

He was profound, my corporal, to say the least.

How do other people do it?

Do you ever find yourself wondering how some people seem to be succeeding in this world and question what they do that is different from you? Do they have a magic formula for life?

The answer is simple – they live by their personal values.

Nobody successful got there by luck, they got there by grit. They succeeded through sheer drive and determination, which in turn was fuelled by what they valued.

They didn't skip training because of the cold and rain. They got up at 6 a.m. instead of having a lie-in. They went to stage school or evening classes when everyone else partied. They studied, wrote and practised day in, day out, fighting all the distractions and feelings that tried to derail them, knowing full well that the easy option didn't exist.

These people are no different from you. All they did was stick to what they value, focusing on the end goal and ignoring the feelings pulling them towards instant gratification.

Anyone who wants to succeed in life must ascend the difficult and demanding re-entrant, not take the easy climb to the west.

Dead in a ditch? You must be joking!

When I was shot at by the enemy for the first time, I momentarily threw all my training out of the window and dived headfirst into a ditch, reacting completely irrationally and not how I had been taught. For a split second I wanted to be curled up on the sofa back at home, allowing someone else to deal with the War on Terror. Yet, when my head appeared back above the water as enemy bullets ripped through the trees above our troop, my mind quickly refocused again on what I stood for.

I wore upon my shoulders material flashes that read 'Royal Marines Commando'. These flashes represented Excellence, Integrity, Self-discipline *and* Humility *– the strong values of a Royal Marine.*

Whenever a clouded moment falls upon a Commando, a simple thought floods the mind: *check your flashes*. We merely cast an eye upon the three words we wear proudly, reminding us of who we are and what we stand for. Just like the inspiration reminder exercise in the last chapter.

During the momentary flinch and desire to hide, I was acting on my need to feel safe, to hide away and seek cowardly comfort in the ditch. But that isn't in our Commando DNA. And, within a split second, I had to remind myself that what I was *feeling* was completely natural, but I had to stay true to my values.

The Commando values gave me the courage to get out of that ditch and into the fight, allowing me to power through the desire to flee, hide and run, and gain the courage to join the battle.

In combat, you cannot make decisions based on how you feel. At every corner or doorway, the instinct for self-preservation is forever present. Intrusive thoughts that insist you think only of yourself and hide.

To ensure we are successful in our missions, we must control ourselves by facing our fears, putting feelings to one side and being guided by our values to work as a team.

Yes, even this . . .

Every comment, every decision, every action you take should reflect your values.

Do I agree with this? Should I say something? Do I believe in that?

Taking a moment to consider your values and choosing to make a decision based on them can sometimes make for testing moments, where there's unease or even tension among your peers. For example, here are some ways that values and feelings can affect your decision-making process:

Are you coming out tonight?	No, I have a book to write. (The value of determination)
	Yeah, why not? I fancy getting drunk! (The feeling)
Fancy a few beers?	No, I am watching my waistline. (The value of health)
	Go on, I've been to the gym once this week! (The feeling)
Let's go shopping.	I'm OK, I am saving. (The value of self-discipline)
	Yeah, I fancy a splurge! (The feeling)
They are rubbish compared with us.	I think they do a worthy job. (The value of humility)
	They are crap; let's tell them! (The feeling)

I'm sure you've had many situations like the examples above where you really want to say yes to something but feel torn by a greater sense of responsibility. Sometimes it's tough to take the hard, sensible route and it can cause awkwardness with your friends, but it's almost always worth that temporary discomfort for the long-term gain. Making decisions using your personal values will ensure you are living true to your principles.

VALUES-BASED DECISION MAKING: 'THE BATTLE'

Winners make decisions based upon their values.

Winners accept they will experience *feelings* from compulsive or irrational thoughts, but own the power to override such thinking. Even when they are down, tired or feel like quitting, winners will remain motivated, taking steps in the direction of their goals – all while using their strong personal values as their driver. I call this the 'values vs feelings battle'.

As I said, feelings aren't always bad. Even your values can sometimes be your downfall. If you take the value 'honesty', for example, being too honest in the wrong places can get you into hot water. Likewise, sometimes acting on feelings when they prompt compassion and love, rather than acting on values of determination or success, will help you grow stronger bonds and more loving relationships.

So, how do you choose what is right or wrong? How do you differentiate between the good and bad decisions?

It's straightforward. When you are about to commit to a decision, you briefly ask yourself whether you are happy and content with the option you're about to choose. Imagine yourself on the other side of the action.

Ask yourself, 'Am I happy and satisfied that I followed that path?'

If yes, you probably made the correct decisions aligned to your values. However, if you feel negativity or resentment following the decision, and find yourself asking, 'Should I be doing this?' then you are more likely to be heading down the wrong pathway.

In times of your own personal values vs feelings battle, it pays to take an extra few seconds or minutes before you commit to a decision, questioning whether the one you are making is the right one. This 'pause over thought' is something we phrase within the marines and the wider military as a 'Condor moment', coined from the Condor tobacco TV adverts of the 1980s.

TAKE A CONDOR MOMENT

Taking a Condor moment is an invaluable process that can greatly clarify your thinking when faced with indecision. It requires you to be aware of the reasons that you're finding this decision hard to make, meaning you must recognize when inappropriate or invasive feelings begin to appear and distract you from your long-term inspirations and goals. When you recognize negative and distracting feelings, this is the process to follow.

—Tool – Condor moment—

When negative feelings kick in – intrusive, annoying, nagging, worrying, compulsive, threatening, irritating, fearful, despairing – the battle has begun.

Pause – Stop and breathe slowly and deeply for one minute. The situation may be pressured or urgent, but taking those vital first few seconds will help you centre yourself. Those extra deep breaths will drive more blood and therefore oxygen to the brain, enabling you to think more clearly.

Think – Now you've paused, think. Keep your mind in the now and begin evaluating your current thoughts and the situation that has presented itself. Put yourself in a conscious state and process exactly how you are feeling. Don't succumb to impulsive behaviours prompted by a spike in your adrenaline. Understand that impulse is normal and allow yourself to process it.

Process – When you have reached this thinking state, begin to process what is positive and negative. Take this moment to remember your inspirations and goals. Why are you doing what you are

---

doing? What is it that has distracted you, and how can it be detrimental to your long-term ambitions? Also consider what the consequences will be of your next actions. Will you regret having the burger, or is there a better alternative? Will you regret going out to the cinema instead of staying in to work on your business plan?

Remind – This is where you align your values. They are your ammunition against whatever it is that has presented itself. Remind yourself of what you stand for and believe in. Values are your compass through uncertain times and this is when you need them most. Are you upholding them? Is the decision you're about to make aligned to them? Will you regret not abiding by them?

Decide – Now it's time to choose. What is your next decision? Use the four steps you have just completed to help you arrive at your decision, and do not be put off by others around you.

Every time you take a Condor moment, you gain clarity and perspective and the decision you make will result in positive outcomes. It will improve your confidence and courage, demonstrating how you can support your inspirations with your values, even when under pressure and under fire.

VALUES ARE THE BACKBONE TO SUCCESS

Your success is built on decisions you have made about your personal values. Stick with them. Although it might not be immediately obvious, staying true to what you believe in will bring great rewards in the long run.

When I took cover in that ditch for the first time, I used a Condor moment to remember who I was and what it meant to be a Royal

Marines Commando, helping me think more clearly. I reminded myself what being a Commando stood for and what it was that I valued.

Sometimes we must make decisions we don't necessarily want to make. Decisions that are difficult, whether personal or professional. It is important that these decisions stem from what you truly value.

Wherever I go as a civilian today, I carry in my wallet a small card stating the Commando ethos, values and spirit. Though I know these off by heart, I still carry them as a gentle reminder of who I am and what I represent, long after my military career. Whenever I hit a hurdle, I can sit down during a Condor moment and look at the card.

Think back to the previous chapter and consider what you chose as your inspirations and the aid you will use to remind you of why you are doing what you are doing.

If your values are true to you and you live by them implicitly, that aid – be it a picture, list or short paragraph – should remind you of what you value, helping guide your future decisions.

As this book progresses, you'll be climbing further up the ICE model, moving into Courage, before Enactment. The next two parts of the ICE model are tough, daunting and often very challenging. However, if you stay true to what you value, you will have the courage to act on your goals and success may come with more ease than maybe you first anticipated.

The value of values

Values are critical in staying aligned to what your heart and mind truly desire.

Values define who you are and what you believe to be important.

Values you own begin to open the doors of opportunity.

Values fine-tune your brain to what you perceive as important.

Values are your moral compass, rules that guide you through life.

Values hold you accountable to what you are working tirelessly towards.

ICE reflection 3:
Cementing your values

By the end of this exercise, you're going to have a clear idea of what your values are.

Put a timer on your phone for two minutes and in that time scribble down as many words as possible that you believe to be your values, or at least reflect who you are, on a page or two of your journal.

Examples might be: *honesty, health, courage, bravery, positivity, family, happiness.*

Look over the list of words. Think of challenges, conflict and adversity you've experienced where certain values and characteristics have leapt to the foreground of your decision making.

Now I want you to ring ten words that stand out to you – that you are drawn to because they might mean a little bit more to you than the rest.

Finally, condense these words down further, to four, five or six core values. To do this, I want you to compare each one of your ten values to the other nine and see which one you think is more important.

So if you had a list of ten words like this below, ask yourself, which is more important to me, health or happiness? Mark a tick next to whichever one you think more important. Then compare the first word to the next word, so health or positivity. Repeat this process until you've worked down the whole list. The words with the most ticks will be your core values. For example:

Health ✓ ✓ ✓ ✓ ✓ ✓
Happiness ✓ ✓ ✓
Positivity ✓ ✓ ✓ ✓ ✓ ✓
Curiosity
Determination ✓ ✓ ✓ ✓ ✓ ✓

Kindness ✓ ✓ ✓ ✓
Courage ✓ ✓ ✓ ✓ ✓ ✓ ✓
Exploration ✓ ✓ ✓
Humility ✓ ✓
Independence ✓ ✓ ✓ ✓

Remember, all of the ten words can be values that you care about and want to live by, but it's important to narrow your focus down to only a few of the most important ones.

Now you've worked out what your core values are, write two or three sentences next to each word describing what they mean to you, why you value them, and why they are the most important values to you.

As you now progress through this book, keep these values at the forefront of your mind.

Break a journey down

Two weeks into Commando training, I am already mentally broken.

'Have I bitten off more than I can chew? Were my friends and family right when they said I'd never make it as a Commando?'

Royal Marines training is eight months of long days, sleepless nights, intense field exercises, physically demanding tests and a constant psychological battle. Of the 245 days, I am only twelve in – I haven't even scratched the surface.

Standing in three ranks as a body of men, our shaved heads, athletic build and tired faces are indistinguishable from each other. We patiently await our instructor.

My feet and legs are aching, tired from the late-night beasting – a term for physical punishment. Some of the recruits are so tired they're having to grab forty winks where they stand. I lock my jaw to suppress another yawn. My eyes bulge with tears of exhaustion, resisting the urge to close.

So far, training has been a blur of late-night ironing, press-ups, confusion and lots and lots of information. Twelve consecutive days seeming like one long one.

'I'm so tired,' I whisper to a lad next to me. 'I'd do anything to get an hour's head down.' He looks straight ahead, with discipline.

'I can't wait to get on that thirty miler and get out of this hell-hole,' I continue.

'OI!' A voice booms across the room. 'WHAT'S YOUR FUCK-ING NAME?'

In my tired state, I've missed our instructor standing to the side, dressed in his immaculately pressed uniform, assessing his troop.

'I said, what is your fucking name, recruit?' he bellows.

Stock still, I'm hoping he's speaking to someone else, ignoring the probability that he's shouting at me.

The clicking of drill boots approaches my side. The instructor appears in my face, with his nose almost touching mine.

''What the fuck is your name?' Now with more menace than before.

'Williams, Corporal,' I whimper.

Looking me up and down, he returns his laser-beam stare to my baggy eyes. 'What were you saying, Williams?' His tone hisses out the last part, my name.

Choking on my throat dried by nerves, I repeat myself. 'I just said I can't wait until the thirty miler, Corporal.'

I momentarily have an out of body experience, standing next to my instructor with folded arms looking back at myself with equal disapproval and disappointment.

What an idiot! I think to myself. *Well done for highlighting your-self so early. So much for staying a grey man!**

The corporal laughs before delivering his cold message. 'You aren't going to survive to the end of the week in this place. Now shut up and start pushing the floor down.' I react swiftly to his command to once again assume the press-up position.

Thirty more weeks of this? I think to myself . . . and for the first and not the last time, the shadowy cloud of doubt creeps in. *I need a better game plan if I am going to survive this course!*

In the excitement and confusion of starting training, I find myself focusing on the finish line that's seven and a half months away, failing to see the mountain I have to climb beforehand. Suddenly, becoming a Royal Marines Commando seems a lot harder.

When my corporal delivers my hard reality check, I decide I'll need to use something more than just my head to get through. This comes in the form of a poster issued to all recruits showing each week of training and the exercises and tests we're required to undertake.

This poster is pinned up on the wall of our six-man room. We decide to cover up all the remaining weeks.

From now on, we will concentrate only on the week we're in, treating each one as the end goal rather than focusing on some far-off, unimaginable end. As each week passes, we celebrate our achievements among ourselves – often over a beer – and then reveal the next week.

We have devised ourselves a system where the long-term goal of gaining a green beret is broken down into manageable short-term goals.

As soon as we do this, it seems as if time is flying.

---

* A 'grey man' is someone who goes unnoticed by the training team.

INSPIRATION

4.
Set Your Goals and
Lay Out the Plan

TRANSFORM YOUR INSPIRATIONS INTO GOALS

When working with clients and speaking to people about my life, I'm often faced with the statement 'I wish I could be as determined as a Commando'. Whenever anyone says this to me, I always reassure them that they are. And you are too. You just might not know how to apply yourself correctly yet.

I recall lying exhausted on my hard, uncomfortable military-issue bed on more than one occasion, staring up at the ceiling, questioning how the hell my life choices had made me end up on the toughest infantry course in the world, not sure if I was up to the challenge. Take faith in the knowledge that, though every marine may own a tough exterior, we have all, deep down, at one point questioned and doubted ourselves.

What makes the marine 'tough' is the interior, not the exterior – the power of their will that convinces them to keep going. And that sometimes comes in a form of strategy, goals and plans. As it did for me.

ONWARDS

At this point in the book, we're going to start thinking about how to turn your hopes and dreams into tangible and viable goals.

Now, you won't be setting goals anything like the targets your boss or manager might ask you to achieve during your annual appraisal. Rather, these goals are about you, driven by your inspirations, and should fill you with motivation and drive. They must be exciting to you, igniting your ambition and determination. The goals you will be setting in the coming chapters are going to slingshot you into a more rewarding and fulfilling life.

You'll be concentrating on what it is you feel you can transform into actual goals. Inspirations such as accumulating wealth or gaining the dream career are quite easy to break down into goals. Others may be a little harder to segment like this, such as starting a family or achieving inner peace. But whatever your ambitions may be, I guarantee that there will be a way to break them down into a series of achievable steps, even if those steps don't appear obvious at first.

Every part of our lives requires the setting of goals in some way or another. They are important targets for us to hit if we are to achieve what we want, within whatever it is that we do. Some of you will already be taking goal-setting seriously, and this chapter won't tell you much you don't already know. Others, however, might be finding the process more challenging. If that is you, the following pages may contain exactly what you have been longing for.

FAILING TO PLAN IS PLANNING TO FAIL

This chapter will help bring your goals to life. You don't necessarily need to plan everything out like a military operation, but it is well worth having a detailed strategy that will guide you towards success. After all, you wouldn't build a house without a blueprint.

Coming from a military background, I am no stranger to a planning procedure or two. Whether in peacetime or at war, I have been witness to planning at all levels. From a three-day training exercise on Dartmoor through to major operations deep in the middle of enemy badlands, planning has always been at the heart of everything.

Good planning is one of the many skills I learned in the Commandos that I find myself bringing to civilian life. My wife rolls her eyes when I plan a trip to the beach like a troop attack on an enemy position. Even a shopping trip has a strategy . . .

- *Write the list in aisle order to minimize foot travel.*
- *Pack seven 'bags for life'.*
- *Ensure two one-pound coins are to hand for a trolley (one for use; one as back-up).*
- *Place two pacifiers in a pocket for the screaming toddler who will likely be present during the operation.*

All joking aside, I have found planning to be the backbone for everything I have done. Writing a detailed business plan and plotting out a road map for my company have been vital to its success, and the planning process for this book was long, extremely detailed and well thought out. Planning is the key to success.

> Planning has made my life far simpler, helping me to clarify my pathway towards success.

BUT WHAT IS A GOAL?

A goal is the solidification of an ambition or dream that will help turn your inspirations into a viable process and plan. Without goals or direction, your inspirations are just ideas that will never reach their full potential direction.

> A goal is your plan, a vision to succeed. It helps turn an idea in your head into an action in the real world. A goal makes the invisible visible.

Goals are a necessity. If you're looking to progress, you must have them in your life. From day-to-day tasks and to-do lists to schedules, programmes and diaries; from big lifetime ambitions to bucket lists – everything becomes centred around your goals. For an entrepreneur, it's their business plan. To the fitness enthusiast, it's a training programme. For a chef, it's the recipe and method.

Write down your goals

In 2007, a study conducted by Dr Gail Matthews of the Dominican University in California demonstrated the importance of goal-setting.

Matthews recruited 267 diverse participants aged from 23 to 72, to identify the difference between goal-setters and non-goal-setters.

Her results indicated that 42 per cent of those who wrote their long-term goals down, and who reported to a friend their progression and successes, ultimately succeeded at what they set.

Matthews's research also identified that those who wrote down short-term goals – and set plans in relation to them – achieved an even greater success rate of 70 per cent.

There are different ways of setting goals and you might already have tried some of them. Some people choose simply to write on a small Post-it note and place it somewhere strategically.

For example, if you want to lose weight, you could choose to place your goals on the biscuit tin or snack cupboard, with a big arrow on it saying *Fruit bowl that way*. At the other end of the scale, you could choose to write out a detailed diet plan, articulating in depth every single calorie-controlled step of the process towards success. It's entirely up to you.

However you set your goals, whether short-term or long, you

must begin to get into the habit of writing them all down with a clear strategy for achieving them.

SHORT-TERM GOALS AND LONG-TERM GOALS

Some of your goals may take several years to achieve while other goals will be reached far sooner. Owning a varied range of goals may mean you'll develop several quite different lists and plans for achieving them.

By definition, short-term goals such as losing five kilos in weight are easier to reach than long-term ones such as gaining a PhD. There's less time between you and the success, meaning your motivation, tenacity and determination will likely be far easier to maintain. They won't be as vigorously tested compared to a long-term goal. The short timeframe also means less room for mistakes, adversity and setbacks, so negativity and doubt will creep in less frequently. On the other hand, the longer you've got, the more there is to worry about and the more time there is to worry!

> Long-term goals require a greater amount of commitment and are likely to be beset with far more problems than your short-term goals.

The longer time stretching between you and your success increases the chances that adversity and setbacks will appear, alongside their partners in crime – negativity and doubt. As a result, maintaining motivation and determination will be more difficult.

One way to overcome this problem is to turn a long-term goal into a series of short-term ones, as my roommates and I did during our Commando training. Instead of dwelling on the intimidating and often overwhelming space between you and success, break it all down into manageable and digestible chunks to maintain momentum and motivation.

Tool – short-term goals for long-term objectives

Goal-setting for some of you will be old news. To others, it will add a whole new and refreshing strategy to your game. Whether you're a goal-setting expert or complete novice, I'd encourage you all to consider the following exercise to help maintain focus and motivation.

- Identify one of your long-term goals and write it down on paper.
- Next to it, write five bullet points on what you could do over the course of a week that will add towards the overall long-term ambition.

For example, your long-term ambition might be to lose weight and shape up. This isn't going to happen overnight and it will take some time for you to achieve the body you desire. But you can progress towards it rapidly if you give yourself short-term goals.

- *Visit the gym three times this week (three bullet points).*
- *Eat healthily and with balance this week (one bullet point).*
- *Lose a kilogram this week (one bullet point).*

Could you implement a similar strategy with one of your long-term goals? You can do this with anything you choose, adding small wins each week into your overall long-term goal. As this will also encourage discipline followed by habit, you'll be teaching yourself to stick with your long-term goals. Why not give it a go?

REVISIT YOUR INSPIRATIONS

Remember, each of your inspirations may contain several long-term goals. And within each long-term goal will lie several short-term goals. Here are just a few examples to get you going, showing how you could break down one of your long-term inspirations or dreams into short-term goals.

Inspiration	Possible goals
Money/Wealth	Outline the dream salary you'd like to earn
	Make a deadline to obtain it
	Create a viable financial plan
Dream career	The actual job title
	Qualification required
	Type of experienced needed
	Place of work
Health/Fitness	Lose/gain weight
	Get fitter
	Find a gym
	Discover diet and training programme
Family	Marry
	Have children
	Dedicate time to family
	Support via career and income
Religion	Attend place of worship set times
	Join certain group
	Practise religion at set times every day/week

SUCCESS BRINGS INTERNAL REWARD

Achieving the goals you've set yourself is an incredible feeling. Achieving one creates an overwhelming sense of pride and joy, gratification and satisfaction. You feel good inside and you are encouraged to do more, to take on the next goal.

These sensations and buzzes of pleasure are a result of four neurological happiness chemicals: endorphins, dopamine, serotonin and oxytocin. These are feelings that matter a great deal. And they've been mattering to humans for a very long time.

Hunter-gatherers did the job

During our primordial years, our ancestors would set out to scavenge and hunt for food to stay alive.

Endless days if not weeks of tracking, stalking, hunting and gathering through adverse weather and treacherous environments to achieve the goal of finding something to eat.

Their reward was more than the food they found: the internal reward of pleasure chemicals.

The food allowed them to physically survive. The four pleasure chemicals made sure they went back out to scavenge and hunt, again and again.

Through evolution, the reason for such chemical rewards has changed, however. Nowadays, these chemical releases are triggered by different habits and behaviours. For example, things that trigger our pleasure chemicals are: physical exercise, sex, love, drugs, checking off to-do lists, securing promotions, getting likes and retweets and ordering fast food, to name a few.

Our lives are easier than the hunter-gather experienced. As a result, the mind and body have adapted the uses of these pleasure chemicals, which are now more commonly associated with feel-good moments sparked from any one of the things in the list above.

When I read about the four pleasure chemicals for the first time in author Simon Sinek's book *Leaders Eat Last* I suddenly, understood myself more. I understood why I fell into using drugs, why

I was drawn to the marines and why I am obsessed with achieving success.

Appreciating how these four chemicals work – and the reasons why they release – will help you accelerate towards success.

Understanding what these four pleasure chemicals are and how they affect your body and mind will help you understand yourself far better during times of indecision or unease.

SO, WHAT ARE THE FOUR PLEASURE CHEMICALS?

ENDORPHINS	OXYTOCIN
The 'runner's high'.	The hug hormone.
Released during exercise, pain, stress and strenuous activity.	The big softy of the four pleasure chemicals.
After exercise, leave you with a euphoric feeling of achievement.	Predominantly responsible for love, friendship, bonding and companionship.
Suppress discomfort and keep you going, acting as the body's own natural pain relief.	Guides the social behavioural functions we require in order to form new relationships.
Surges of endorphins are commonly released during laughter, helping to remove stress and anxiety.	Your biggest friend when creating closer and tighter groups of people.
When you're down and upset, people will often try to cheer you up, so you can activate your endorphins and replace unwanted feelings.	Useful in a more innovative strategy that involves bringing people together, creating ways of getting them to secrete the friendly hormone, as they build better relationships.

SEROTONIN	DOPAMINE
The confidence molecule.	The motivation chemical.
Provides feelings of pride, significance and status.	It's the feeling of 'Yes I did it!'

Encourages us to go out and seek recognition from others like Mum and Dad, boss or friend.	It's that happy reward moment you get on completion of a task, naturally boosting drive, focus and concentration.
Fills us with delight when we succeed, especially when other people see us do it.	Makes us competitive, often providing that feeling of achievement; like our ancestors received when they succeeded in a scavenge or hunt.
As well as fuelling self-confidence, it's responsible for those chin-up-and-puff-out-your-chest moments that make you feel good.	Keeps us driven towards success, goal planning and raising ambitions as we progress.

In everything that we do

As soon as I learned about the four pleasure chemicals I saw them cropping up in daily life, and when I looked back at my career in the Royal Marines, I saw them in everything that we did.

When I was exhausted in battle it was my endorphins that suppressed the pain and kept me powering through. I can recall how dopamine made me feel good after completing a difficult and sometimes unrelenting task. How oxytocin bonded inseparable relationships between my comrades and me. I remember the feelings of serotonin at the end of my recruit training; and later, whenever anyone asked what I did for a living and I'd beam with pride as I told them I was a Royal Marines Commando.

— Pause for thought —

I want to encourage you to reflect on moments in life when you too can recall feeling the effects of some of these chemicals.

It may be the birth of your children, passing an exam, finishing a race, completing a challenge or landing a contract.

Write each chemical as a heading in your journal and under each one put down a time that you experienced it. Identify where these chemicals show up in your life and keep them at the front of your mind.

BE DRIVEN BY THE END FEELING

Ever found yourself saying 'I'd give that another go' after fulfilling something that once filled you with dread and worry? Perhaps it was a 10k run, delivering a speech at a friend's wedding or presenting to hundreds of people at a conference. On completion of a task, the fear and anxiety you were feeling are suddenly replaced with happiness and pride, elation and gratification.

Our pleasure chemicals are predominantly responsible for these sudden turns in outlook. A mother's extreme pain induced by childbirth almost instantly subsides as she feels and smells her incredible creation for the first time, oxytocin binding unconditional love in a single second.

For the marathon runner, pain from the continuous impact of bone on tarmac for hours on end disappears at the finish line as endorphins kill the agony.

Dopamine bubbles up within as the driving examiner says, 'You've passed!' or when you receive that phone call after months of waiting to say that the job is yours.

Serotonin oozes through as you catch a reflection of yourself proudly wearing the medal you've worked so hard to win.

After any achievement like this the worry and pain subside and are replaced by feelings of pride, joy, happiness and success.

The four pleasure chemicals are your reward for demonstrating how capable you truly are.

Knowing about these chemicals and how they impact you will affect how you approach each of your goals, and motivate you towards fulfilling them.

You will own a greater understanding of what your mind and body are experiencing, arming you with the powerful knowledge that, whatever it is you face, there will be internal rewards as a by-product of your success. When you're struggling to make progress or shying away from a challenge, just remember how good you're going to feel when you get through to the other side. Staying inside warm and cosy on a Saturday morning might feel nice, but the feeling you get from returning from a 5k run is even nicer!

PLAN WITH THESE CHEMICALS IN MIND

When you can identify how you're naturally reacting to success, why not bottle it up and use it?

Once you get hooked on these four pleasure chemicals, happiness and success suddenly seem far more achievable – and the completion of your goals more accessible.

So, now you appreciate the four pleasure chemicals and how they improve human behaviour, we need to make the link between what they are and how they can benefit your goals. It's also important to establish how they should be considered within your planning.

Making the link is relatively simple and comes from thinking ahead, particularly about how you're *going to feel*.

Cast your mind back to earlier in the chapter and think again about how short-term goals are easier to stay motivated for than long-term ones.

Game plan for pleasure

Your pleasure chemicals bring you internal reward, self-generated feel-good factors that help maintain your drive and motivation. So it would be wise in your planning phase to consider this thought and find a way to make these human 'chemical drug hits' more regular.

You have your long-term goals, inspirations you want to achieve within your lifetime, but they may seem very far away. If there seems to be little reward in return for your hard work now, your passion and desire, drive and motivation may diminish over the years.

This is one of the main reasons why you should plan lots of short-term goals into your long-term ones, allowing yourself more exposure to mini successes, which ultimately trigger these four happy neuro bursts.

You want to make your journey on the path towards success as rewarding as possible. Otherwise, your passion and desire are likely to burn out and you will swiftly find yourself losing sight of the end goal.

> As I did in recruit training, break a journey down and find ways of providing yourself with regular shots from the four pleasure chemicals to keep you going.

During training, every time we reflected on the week we'd just completed, before revealing the next week's schedule to ourselves, we celebrated finishing another week and it felt so good that it kept us focused.

You too should apply an identical strategy to your own game plan and maintain your pathway to success with lots of regular achievement-driven hits of pleasure. To make this even easier to do and keep you on track you could write the chemical you're going to generate under your short-term goal. So when you're planning your week, and you write yourself a goal to get you one step closer to your dream, underneath it write the amazing feeling you'll experience. This will make you more likely to do it!

FIVE STEPS IN PLANNING A GOAL

There are thousands of experts across the world who claim to have created the most effective goal-planning strategy, some of whom amass a fortune by teaching it. Though often similar, there are so many strategies and approaches available that the choice can feel overwhelming. People often worry whether they've picked the right or wrong one to follow.

If this is you, don't worry. In my opinion, there's no right or wrong way to approach goal-setting, it is a matter of personal preference. Success in goal-setting boils down to finding the right strategy for you.

I have spent years reading books, listening to podcasts and audio books, watching motivational videos and TED talks on YouTube, researching the best way to set goals, trying to discover what the best way is. While I'd always encourage you to go and find out for yourself, I've done a lot of this research so you don't have to. I have pulled everything I have learned into five steps.

To make things simpler, in Step Three below I have drawn upon the SMART plan, a simple, easy-to-use model to build your goals from that I came across a lot throughout my career. However, if you prefer a different method, feel free to replace the SMART planner with something more relevant to you.

SMART stands for:

- Specific – What are the specific details of your goal, and can it be broken into smaller steps?
- Measurable – Can you measure performance and record data using a calendar, an app, etc.
- Achievable – Is the goal attainable and within your ability to complete?
- Relevant – Is the goal worthwhile to you? Do you actually want it?
- Timebound – Set a sensible deadline. You won't lose three stone overnight, but you might over three months.

Familiarize yourself by reading through them. I've summarized your writing tasks in ICE reflection 4 at the end of the chapter, when you're going to write out your own strategy. For now, though, just read through each step and start thinking about how it applies to your goals and ambitions.

STEP ONE – Pick a goal that motivates you

Actions	Supporting thoughts
Write down everything you want to achieve on one page of your journal – your biggest aspirations and long-term goals.	If you have followed the ICE reflections at the end of each chapter, you'll already have a list of things you want to achieve in your Commando mindset journal.
Then use each goal as a heading on a blank page of your journal, leaving a minimum of five or six pages between them – you're going to need the space later.	I'm hoping your goals are etched in your mind, but if they aren't, revisit your journal.

When you set your New Year's resolutions, how far do you get? Are they impulsive, champagne-cheering irrational decisions? Or are they meaningful? How far have you got? How many of your resolutions have you ever actually kept?

Many people who pick a New Year's resolution do it off the cuff – an irrational decision. There is often little meaning behind them and rarely any passion; just a spur-of-the-moment goal we think we ought to be aiming for. This is what the average person does.

But you're not average. You are different. Your goals are solid. You've got them down on paper. The first tactic has been employed.

STEP TWO – Set the date and calculate the timeline

Actions	Supporting thoughts
Decide on when you want to achieve these goals by, and plot the dates. Be specific – use a calendar.	Confirm to yourself that the time you set is both reasonable and achievable.
Then calculate how many days you have remaining to complete each one.	Be honest with yourself and ensure you're not biting off more than you can chew in a short space of time.

Write these figures down next to the goal and corresponding date in your journal.

Some of your goals will be well over a year away, so plotting the exact date and calculating their days will be trickier – but do your best.

NOTE: You have just mapped out your path to success. Though you know you have several long-term goals maybe a few years out, you've now scheduled those short-term goals you can meet this year and how long you have to complete each one. You've created focus along your path and prioritized each goal.

STEP THREE – Set your goal recipe using a SMART plan

Actions	Supporting thoughts
For each goal, think about the ingredients you need in order to turn your goal into a reality. Write out a recipe for success for each goal.	Ingredients – What is it made of? Resources – What is required to make it?
Under each one of your goals, write out a more specific strategy using the SMART plan.	Time – How long will it take? Method – How will it be made? Your goals may be varied, each requiring a different strategy. Here are some qualities to consider when using the SMART plan: **S**pecific What is the actual goal? (In one sentence) How often do you need to work on it? (Daily, weekly, monthly, yearly?) Where will it take place? (Home, gym, work, school?) **M**easurable How will you see and note your progression? (Have something to record your progression)

Set waypoints: short-term goals to evaluate how you are performing. (Business growth chart, fitness recordings, progress charts)

Achievable

You must be motivated and inspired by your goals, but they should also be attainable.

Don't strive for something you know in your heart you will never achieve.

Be honest with yourself and your ability in reaching them.

Relevant

Set your goals for you, not for someone else.

They must be relevant to you and centred around your inspirations; don't strive for someone's else's ambition.

Timebound

Set dates and times for achieving your goals.

Allow yourself realistic, achievable timeframes.

This recipe doesn't need to be overly detailed, just a rough outline of your requirements. You can set out each goal using this simple methodology.

The recipe is purposely vague, so you have to think deeply about each goal and what you're going to need. You need to put thought into each one, you can't have it all on a plate, if you'll excuse the pun!

Once you've taken the time to consider a recipe for each of your goals, you can construct a more detailed strategy using a SMART plan or similar.

Take your time when doing this. Be as detailed as you can. The clearer and more directed you are, the better.

STEP FOUR – Break each long-term goal into several short-term goals

Actions	Supporting thoughts
Break each or your goals down into more manageable and digestible chunks.	Use your knowledge of the important difference between long- and short-term goals.
For every short-term goal, follow Steps One to Three, writing them down and thinking about SMART.	You'll need those extra pages I told you to leave back at Step One.
Buy a wall planner and write on it the deadlines for your short-term goals.	

Taking the time to go through the strategy again for each short-term goal may seem galling at first, but it will pay off.

You'll find that your dreams look much more manageable as you break things down in a microscopic way. It may seem like there's a lot to do, but get the planning correct and you'll stand a far greater chance of succeeding in your mission.

STEP FIVE – Share the journey with a friend

Action	Supporting thought
Add some accountability to what you're doing – share your intentions and aspirations with a trustworthy friend.	Share what it is you will achieve and when you want to achieve it by.

Sharing your goals is something I urge you to do. If you feel nervous about sharing your goals, make sure you pick someone you will feel comfortable talking to about them. Bear in mind that they might not be as passionate about those goals as you are and might not care to know the intricate details of your plan or step-by-step process but they should be encouraging about your overall aim.

The benefits of sharing your goals is that you will be conscious of the fact someone else knows what you plan to achieve, and you will therefore feel more motivated to make it happen, and also when doubt, negativity, or quitting enter your mind, the person you choose to share your ambition with can act as a reminder to keep going.

Equally, you might well be doing them a favour. Many confidants feel spurred on to do the same, possibly joining you and writing down their own goals and sharing them with you. You could inspire someone to make a change in their own life.

— Morning and evening goal reminder —

I'd like you to get your hands on a very small notepad – the size of a big matchbox – and place it by your bed, or in a drawer near where you sleep.

Every morning and evening take this notepad and scribble down your most important goals – or all of them if you want. This will help you maintain focus every day, and keep your goals and inspirations always at the front of your mind.

Waking up and being greeted by them and revisiting them before going to sleep will help you act on them.

ICE reflection 4:
Goals to plans

Earlier in the chapter, I asked you to write out one of your ambitions and break it down into a few small steps you could achieve that week.

Now, on a new page of your journal, draw the structure of the five steps – and translate each of your ambitions into several long-term goals.

Break down each of those long-term goals, into short-term goals.

Begin placing these long- and short-term goals into a time-frame, marking when you'll complete each by and who you'll share the goals with.

Go back over the five-step process and use it to plan each ambition you'd like to work on.

Then, prepare for action. The next part of this book is where it gets real and we gain the courage to turn our dreams into reality.

COURAGE

Courage is the most important of all the virtues because, without courage, you can't practise any other virtue consistently.
Maya Angelou

Metres from the enemy

Rounds ricochet off the rooftops, inches from guys firing at the approaching enemy.

'They're moving through the treelines north and west of our position,' someone shouts.

The end of their message is drowned out by the whoosh of an RPG before it explodes on the other side of the compound wall.

I peer upwards through one eye as the intense glow of the sun burns at my vision. I'm conscious I'm standing where five of our men were hit by a similar grenade earlier today – some of their kit and blood still strewn across the dusty floor.

I watch the fight ensue. There's little room for all of us on the roof. With some resentment, I look on as my friends risk their lives in the heat of the battle.

Crack-crack-crack-crack-crack! More enemy rounds travel metres from their heads.

'It looks like they're surrounding us!' the same voice yells down. 'They're fucking flanking us!'

Thud! Thud! Two loud explosions ring out, on the other side of the wall, metres away.

'They're gonna have a go here, I think, boss!' Ben Willmott, one of our corporals, shouts in his thick Welsh accent to our captain, 'Mad Mac', who himself is calmly radioing updates into HQ.

'Excuse me. He's right, they are flanking us.' A soft Afghan voice interrupts us both as we look to the roofs. Turning simultaneously, we see our interpreter, who is looking worried.

'Say again, mate?' Willmott asks. 'What do you mean?' he adds with some concern.

'I have been listening to their messages,' says the interpreter. 'They are going to use the treeline that leads up to the compound as cover. And break in.'

Fuck me! I think to myself. *Break in?*

From a patrol earlier today, I know exactly the treeline they're using. And it leads right up to the gate Willmott and I are standing by.

The interpreter continues. 'They are using the cover from the crops and the water behind that treeline to get up close.' He points through the gate in the direction of the stream as he says this.

Willmott begins yelling to the roofs, 'Lads, can you see anyone in the nearest treeline?'

But it's noisy. The guys are preoccupied with incoming fire, missing what he said.

Turning my sight from the roof to the gate, all I can imagine is Taliban fighters on the other side, readying themselves to bomb-burst in bearing grenades and AK-47s, wearing a sinister and fixated look of death in their eyes.

Willmott grabs my arm and I follow him, unaware of where we're heading.

'Boss, I think they're coming up to the gate, over there,' he suggests to our captain. 'Let me take Ben and we'll hose the nearest field and treeline.'

My eyes bulge as I begin processing what Willmott has said. 'Mad Mac' drags slowly on a cigarette, savouring every bit of nicotine, before giving the nod to Willmott.

'To the gate!' orders my commander.

At the gate, pressing myself into the wall next to it, I look down to see Willmott's hand gripping the handle.

'OK. I'm going to swing it open. And, as I do, I want you to sprint out and aim at the treeline. Empty all your ammunition into the trees and the edge of the field. Then get back in.'

Processing his words, I reluctantly swallow on a dry throat, before cautiously nodding.

'Happy?' asks Willmott.

Is that a fucking rhetorical question?

I confidently nod again at his command. Yet, deep down, I feel sick.

I'm about to step from the relative safety of our compound during a Taliban attack, potentially into their sights as they lie only metres away from us, awaiting their command to enter our compound.

'No, I ain't fucking happy!' I want to say. But I keep that comment to myself.

Sweating profusely, my hands begin struggling with the weight of my weapon. As it slips through my greasy palms, my fingers dig in to stay in control.

Pausing for a moment, I notice my breathing is fast and my heart rate even quicker. And I suddenly recognize the adrenal response I've become so used to.

Yet today, it seems far more overwhelming. Is fear taking a grip of me? I'm accustomed to the 'fight-or-flight' response. But now, more than ever, my legs are trying to run in a different direction from my weapon.

'Get ready. Three . . .'

Willmott's hand begins turning the gate handle. I grip my weapon tightly.

'. . . Two . . .'

All my muscles are stiffening, priming themselves to deliver extreme but calculated violence in a split second.

'. . . One.'

Switching my weapon's safety to fire, I kick the gate clear before stepping through, instantly taking aim and beginning to fire.

My finger is locked down on the trigger of my light machine gun as it spits out tens of rounds a second in a flash of flame.

Aiming through the tunnel vision of my weapon's sight, I lay fire into the treeline metres to our front.

Marines fire from the roofs. Willmott shoots alongside me. I'm shielded behind a protective wall of hot lead spraying at our foes.

I feel alive. The fear has gone, replaced by a sense of immortality.

I am exposed, but completely in control. I have been trained for this moment.

Those who are sneaking up on us are more than likely back-pedalling for cover.

My weapon violently shakes my body as I empty its ammunition into the vegetation and stream.

The trees are dense. Only the crashing sound of people quickly wading through water and snagging on branches identifies that anyone is even there.

We aren't letting up. Willmott and I continue shooting, sending a message. 'Do not try your dirty tactics on us again!'

My gun suddenly stops firing.

Briefly lost in the moment of an overwhelming adrenaline high, I have forgotten to monitor my ammunition, becoming so fixated on killing the enemy that I have overlooked its depletion.

I'm defenceless and immediately feel very vulnerable.

Within a split second my immortal, godlike feeling diminishes. I'm suddenly more like a cowering little boy, alone in a playground waiting for the bullies to get him.

'Stoppage!' I scream out to Willmott, while dropping to my knees to reload another belt.

Fuck! I hope the Taliban can't understand English. They'll immediately turn around, knowing I'm now an easy target.

Swiftly, the world shifts against me.

My ammunition pouch won't open. When it does, I fumble with the new belt of 5.56mm rounds now snagging on my kit. Eventually, I clumsily load them into my weapon.

I know my gun intimately. And I'm still being quick. But, in this situation, even a tiny delay makes a huge difference. *Pull yourself together, Ben!*

Bang! Bang! Bang! Gunfire echoes next to me, hurling my attention back into the action, as Willmott appears in my periphery, firing accurately at our targets.

'Get inside!' he shouts. So I turn and dash for the compound.

There's firing everywhere now. Outgoing from the roofs. And Willmott. Incoming from the Taliban. It's utter carnage, difficult to make out who is shooting at whom.

Pulling my head out of my arse, I cock my weapon as I move back to the compound, take aim and let rip another violent burst at our enemy.

'BEN, MOVE!' I yell at Willmott, letting him know he can abandon his position and sprint for the compound.

'MOVING!' he shouts back. And I cover his movement with bursts of fire, allowing him to turn his back on the enemy for a few seconds.

Willmott dashes past me into the compound. After one final roar of my weapon, he slams the gate shut.

COURAGE

↑

INSPIRATION

5.
Face Your Fears

Would you be courageous enough to walk into a room full of people you didn't know, dressed as Batman or a Smurf, while declaring your favourite dinosaur to be a diplodocus? Probably not, yet it's the kind of thing you wouldn't have given a second thought when you were a child. Does that make children more courageous than adults?

Some argue that humans are born with courage, others say that it is taught and developed. Yet, when you consider we are born with only two fears – of falling and of noise – it would indicate that we surely *must* all be born with courage.

I agree with both sentiments – we are born with courage, but we can also develop it as we grow.

Courage (noun) The ability to do something that frightens you – also known as bravery; the ability to remain strong in the face of pain or grief.

In the Royal Marines courage is developed through training and immersion into difficult and often testing simulated situations. Commando training is both physically and mentally challenging, meaning recruits must continuously draw upon their courage to get through.

Long hours spent on exhausting marches carrying heavy loads across barren land in adverse weather conditions isn't designed just to annoy recruits. Training is tough for a reason. It is done to expose the potential marines to themselves. They learn to understand their bodies and minds when they are depleted and exhausted, discovering how much more they can endure.

We are continually asking the recruits to be more courageous. Even when training is complete, courage is something every marine will have to act upon as they progress through their careers. Whether delivering a lecture to their peers on a course or fighting doorway to doorway in the battlespace, we are always asked to push ourselves that little bit more each time. Courage is one of our core values, a word we express as, *get out front and do what is right*.

COURAGE IN THE ICE MODEL

You are now entering the second stage of the ICE model – designed to build upon your courage.

All of you have courage. You would not be in the position you are in life right now without it. You needed courage to take your exams at school, go for a job interview, or pick up a book titled *Commando Mindset*.

Anyone can sit at home, dreaming of what it is they want to achieve in life. From your sofa, it's easy to transform your inspirations into goals and imagine where you could be one day if only you applied yourself. But it takes courage to actually make that happen.

> It takes more than imagination and desire to transform your goals into reality and enact the plan. To make it all come to life takes courage.

On fear

During our coaching, whenever we discuss courage, we talk about fear. Fear is a feeling. Because of it, many people fall at the first hurdle towards enactment. Plagued with doubt and worry, concern and angst, people allow fear to take control of their destiny, and run away from it rather than facing it.

However, the sooner you understand fear and why your mind and body feel as they do during certain situations, the sooner you'll learn to embrace it and the sooner you'll be able to open a new world of success.

— Pause for thought —

Think of a time in your life when you let fear take control, and prevent you from doing something you *wanted* to do.

Ask yourself why this happened. What was it that caused you to stop in your tracks? Was it the feeling of fear itself, or the possibility of what *might* happen, what *could* go wrong?

FEAR COMPLEMENTS COURAGE

Fear (noun) A distressing emotion aroused by impending danger, evil, pain, etc., whether the threat is real or imagined; the feeling or condition of being afraid.

In Chris Terrill's hit Channel 5 documentary *Royal Marines: Mission Afghanistan*, Terrill followed our Royal Marines company (Lima Company) for several weeks on operations. He reported that the area we were operating in was the most IED-infested in Afghanistan. He aptly described the ground around our base as 'the most dangerous square mile in the world'.

We took on average two to three major casualties a week at CP Toki – our remote checkpoint in Helmand – mostly from the hidden explosives. Every step we took outside the base had the potential to be our last. We were risking life and limb in order to seek change for the local people, who had endured such conflicts for the previous fifty years.

It was never lost on me that under every foot placement could be the IED with my name on it. Or that I was always potentially in the enemy's sights.

Out on patrol, our interpreter would forever be feeding us information about the Taliban, by way of his handheld radio, which he tuned to the enemy's frequencies. 'They can see us now.' 'They will hit us on the next track.' 'They say we are heading towards the IED.'

Afghanistan was just a constant mental battle – a 'head fuck', we called it.

Sometimes, the easiest moments were in battle, where the mind could focus on the most primitive human behaviour – the fight for survival.

The hardest battle of all was controlling the fear, which grew with every new intelligence report of more enemy in our area, every warning about hidden IEDs, every interpreter's intercepted message and, of course, the constant threat of walking into our foe's gunsights.

However, in Commando training, it was always made clear to us that fear adds caution to courage – we understood that fear actually gave us the edge when we needed one most.

We would repeatedly practise controlling ourselves through simulated stressful situations and scenarios that would induce fear. Rehearsing how not to allow intrusive thoughts to cloud our judgement when the real event prevailed.

Much of our training is difficult to replicate in the civilian world.

I would suggest going into a CS gas-filled chamber and removing your gas mask to test yourself during a chemical attack will not be of much use if all you want to do is learn how to salsa. And running ten kilometres in full kit followed by a shooting test is not going to help you get that next promotion.

However, you can learn from how we act courageously in the face of fear. In the same way that we walked into that CS gas chamber, the next time you need to resolve a conflict with a colleague, go and speak directly to them rather than avoiding them or resorting to email to solve the issue.

FACING YOUR FEARS

Fear can never be eradicated. It is biologically programmed into you to ensure you stay alert and safe during times of threat. But it can be controlled, and even used to your advantage.

Success does not come with ease, but by overcoming adversity and challenge, and owning an ability to face your biggest worries.

Every journey involves difficulty and doubt, yet those who dare step into the fray, allowing themselves to overcome the mind's taunts of failure or worry, are far more likely to succeed.

> You too will have stood at your own compound gate, preparing for it to open, unaware of what awaits you on the other side.

In the pursuit of success, fear will always be present. You will need to face fear regularly if you want to take your life to the next level. You can do it. You have the courage.

—Exercise: List your fears—

In your journal, start a new section for Courage.
Write out a short list of your fears.

Think hard; don't rush.

Consider what first jumped to mind during the last 'Pause for thought' on page 115.

Don't overcomplicate what you choose and try to stay as everyday as you can. Bungee jumps or flying aren't an everyday occurrence for the majority of us, so try and pick something that happens a bit more frequently. (Of course, if you happen to be a fearful flight attendant or bungee-rope demonstrator, feel free to crack on!)

Is it picking up the phone to someone? Having a difficult chat with a member of your team? Applying to a gym for the first time? Or filling out that application?

For each fear you have, write down why you fear it.

Pick just one for now that is affecting you regularly, and that you would really like to see resolved. Something you can face daily that will draw out your courage.

Now elaborate on this fear by adding a bit more detail about *why* you fear it. What precisely is it about this situation that makes you feel as you do? Understanding why you fear something will help you overcome it. Being able to control and harness fear helps you grow your courage.

This ability stems from acceptance and admittance, so be honest with yourself.

When you are done giving reasons, list two or three positive steps you can take now that will help you to overcome this fear.

Moving forward, try implementing some of these changes in the coming days.

FIGHT, FLIGHT OR FREEZE

Being afraid or fearing something isn't a weakness. Depending on the choices you make during moments of unease, it's a challenge that exposes your true character. Some will stand and fight their fears, others will flee.

First described by American physiologist Walter Bradford Cannon in 1915, the fight-or-flight response (acute stress response) is a physiological reaction that occurs during a perceived threat to survival. When you feel threatened, you'll make the decision – fight or flight – in a split second.

When people first hear about this, they usually think of a physical threat, such as a mugger in an alleyway. Would they run away or confront them? Yet the fight-or-flight response is far less animalistic and more commonplace than that. It can occur even in day-to-day occurrences, such as the decision to walk away from an office dispute or get involved in a slanging match. Or, comically, running indoors when a threatening wasp aims for your cake rather than choosing to swipe at it. We are always in fight-or-flight mode, without even realizing it.

But there's a third, very different reaction, which is to freeze – simply not to do anything at all. In freeze mode, picture that unlucky rabbit caught in the headlights, watching the car hurtle towards it as it stays rooted to the spot.

For marines in combat it's imperative to know how to act swiftly and not succumb to shock. This might mean diving for cover in a hail of bullets to assess the next move (flight) or advancing swiftly into the fray (fight). Freezing is simply not an option.

Why do we freeze?

Fortunately for the timid rabbit, freezing is usually followed by a more positive decision to run away (flight).

A predator such as a lion, on the other hand, might also freeze when startled, but in most cases the next decision will be to attack (fight).

These are natural behaviours throughout the animal kingdom, including humankind.

Among fight, flight or freeze, the most common behaviour is to freeze. Mouth open, feet planted, immobile.

Are you someone who freezes?

When it comes to your fears, have you experienced moments in which you stand and face the fear, or do you turn and run every time? Or are you, like most people, trapped between both? Indecisive? Frozen?

Do you recognize the reasons that have held you back, restricting you from reaching your maximum potential?

All of us have fears that can prompt these reactions. You may be someone who becomes overwhelmed and starts to panic; your palms sweat, your cheeks flush; perhaps you even start to lose control in the face of fear, crying or unable to talk. Or you may be someone who looks cool and calm on the surface, yet in whom tension bubbles like a volcano.

When I stepped out of the gate with Ben Willmott, our mission was to succeed. Getting out of our compound, standing and fighting the enemy and surviving – that was our goal. And I needed courage to make it happen. I accepted my fears, felt the physical reflexes they induced, and I acted despite them, as did Ben.

To help us avoid both the freeze and flight responses, it's helpful to think about the long-term impact of not facing up to our fears. Actively avoiding something can seem trivial at the time, but it may have devastating impact on your future. Letting another week go by without picking up the phone and speaking with that estranged family member might seem easy now, but could have a detrimental effect on your future relationship.

What about putting off that difficult conversation with a team member? It makes life easier now to avoid it, but how much more of an impact will it have on your team's or organization's performance? Think of the long-term impact of your response to fear.

PHYSICAL SYMPTOMS OF FEAR

When you're afraid – and fight, flight or freeze mode triggers – your brain immediately accelerates a chain of events that leads to your quick decision-making response. All within a split second.

When fear is perceived, the amygdala – a very early evolutionary thinking engine deep within your brain – sends signals to your nervous system that stimulate your muscles. You get a feeling of tension and tightness, as if readying for combat.

A hormonal response activates your adrenal system; stress hormones – cortisol, adrenaline (epinephrine) and noradrenaline (norepinephrine) – are released into your bloodstream; these are responsible for your body's speed, strength and alertness, priming it to its full potential, ready for when you choose to engage with the situation, or run.

A neural response activates the sympathetic nervous system . . .

- *increasing* your breathing . . .
- *speeding up* heart rate . . .
- *starting* sweating as a system coolant . . .
- *moving* the material in your large intestine . . .
- *dilating* the pupils . . .
- *raising* your blood pressure.

Just thinking about what you fear will start this process of bodily acceleration. These are all normal responses and they are often misinterpreted as bad signs rather than signs that your body is ready and helping you to work through the fear. Understanding how your body responds to fear, even if only a minimal understanding like mine, will assist you in thinking clearly in moments of stress.

Someone with a Commando mindset will accept and understand that what you are feeling is normal. When such feelings and sensations arise, they indicate that a dangerous or difficult situation is about to occur. Being aware of them and the reason behind them is half the battle in controlling yourself.

'These sensations are normal, and I can still complete the task.'

'I will not allow my body to get the better of me.'

'I am in fear. I do want to run. But I know I must commit.'

The more opportunity you have to be saying sentences like these in your head (or even out loud if need be), the more control you will gain over yourself.

WHAT IF I SUCCEED?

When facing a big challenge, doubts and worry will always creep in. When getting close to doing something that helps us towards our goal, we might start asking ourselves questions like:

- 'What if they think badly of me?'
- 'What if I fail?'
- 'What if I make a mistake?'
- 'What if I lose?'
- 'What if I die?'

But you must overcome these negative feelings, turning the defeatist 'what ifs' into 'What if I succeed?' You must just go through the gate, train your brain to think more positively and imagine the best-case scenario instead of the worst. As well as replacing thoughts about failure with visions of success – and perhaps more importantly – ask yourself what would happen if you shied away from the task altogether.

Transform 'What if I fail?' into 'What if I don't even try?'

By switching your perspective to think about how you would feel if you didn't do something you'll feel inspired to work through the fear, because often the regret inspired by not doing something is much bigger than the pain of trying and failing. When next faced with fear, understanding what's happening in your mind will make the difference during decision making. Such knowledge will help you deliver your speech, take the exam, leave your partner, find a partner, slot home the penalty, step into the ring, complete the application form, quit your job, start up a business or make your first skydive.

Your body's reaction to fear will never go away, and you wouldn't want it to, but you can learn to understand and control certain responses that can help you make better decisions. Doing so will bring clarity to every fight, flight or freeze moment you encounter. Accept that the fear exists and move on. Make fear your friend and then walk through the gate with it.

A COMMANDO ATTITUDE TO FEAR?

Going back to my experience at the compound gate, I had no choice in the matter. I had to go through that gate. It was my job. Refusal was not an option.

This meant I had to face my fears and expose myself once more to the realities of war. Kill or be killed. We all had to. Every single one of us was afraid in one way or another. But we had to get the job done. Lives were at stake.

In response, I had to harness the physiological responses and apply myself to the task. Otherwise, I would definitely have crumbled. Bone-white knuckles, gripping my weapon, I knew the fear I was experiencing was natural. I had been in similar situations before. My reactions were normal.

As you begin to act on some of your goals, you may face intimidating moments when you have to put yourself out there and risk your reputation, your money or even your life. In order to do that, you need to overcome your fears.

Harnessing your fears is one of the most difficult things to do. But once you do, any challenge will seem achievable. Doors to worlds will suddenly open further and you'll be exposed to opportunities you once thought were unreachable.

ICE reflection 5:
Help someone else build courage

Now, this may seem a bit different, as it's all been about you up until this point – and rightly so.

However, for this ICE reflection, I want you to concentrate on someone else, or at least work alongside them.

Earlier in the chapter, I asked you to list your fears and identify what may worry you or cause doubt.

Now, pick someone close to you and get them to write their own list.

As long as you are both comfortable with doing so, share your lists and identify any fears that you may have in common.

Of those fears that are similar, pick just one you both share and agree on. This is the fear you are going to tackle together.

Give yourselves a sensible deadline to overcome this fear and log the date. To add that extra bit of accountability, both of you should sign under the date.

Now go for it. Together, begin exposing yourself to this fear and encourage one another to push through it. It may be holding a spider. It could be public speaking. Skydiving. Starting a conversation with a stranger.

Record how you get on and watch each other's courage grow.

Within the marines, courage didn't just stem from our own abilities, skills and beliefs, but also from trusting those around us who are equally, if not more, skilled.

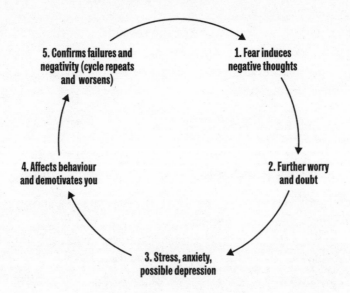

If you want to make fear your friend, get your sleep right

Ever woken in the morning after falling asleep stressed or in the grip of something that causes you worry, feeling more drained than you felt the night before?

Such thoughts trigger the same biological adrenal reactions you'd experience during moments of fear. If you don't take charge of them, positively controlling and harnessing your fears will become far harder.

To embody the Commando mindset you will be required to use fear as a strength. Allowing fear to engulf your thoughts when you should be resting, has the opposite effect to what you want.

If you lose sleep to fear, you expose yourself to the threat of becoming locked in a negative cycle, in which your fear controls you.

Tips for a fear-free sleep

Try this evening/night-time routine and see if it reduces your stress levels and fatigue:

- Get thirty to forty minutes' exercise in the day, preferably in the morning, to stimulate your body and tire yourself naturally. Try not to exercise less than two hours before you intend to go to bed.
- Avoid eating anything two or three hours before you intend to sleep.
- Avoid blue screen electronics an hour before bed.
- Meditate. Twenty minutes is all you need, lying on your bed with your earphones plugged in, listening to one of the millions of podcasts or apps available online. Meditating brings you into a present state and away from distracting thoughts.

- Have a thirty-second <u>cold shower</u> an hour before bed. Tricking your body into releasing melatonin is only going to make you nod off quicker.
- Become a bookworm. Try <u>reading</u> a few chapters of a gripping novel to get a better night's sleep. (Note: it's widely believed that non-fiction is more stimulating to the mind, whereas fiction helps you drift off. So put down *Commando Mindset* and pick up a page-turner at night time!)

Courage comes in many forms

Another patrol, another day in paradise – warzone style!

We've spent several hours among a cluster of compounds, demonstrating to the locals our presence and determination in keeping the Taliban at bay, providing for their security.

'Hello Zero, Hello Zero. This is One-One Alpha. That's us now firm in Compound 82.'

The boss's voice is low, radioing our position into HQ. Sitting in the courtyard below, he studies his map with Zach, assessing where best to head next.

Lying on the roof above, in an overwatch position, I notice there's calm in the air. The troop seems relaxed.

Those not providing security are unwinding, slumped in areas of shade, grabbing some respite.

The compound owner seems unperturbed by our presence.

The landscape before me is lush with small trees – feeling more like a vineyard than a violent warzone.

Regular sounds of helicopters, firefights and explosions have been replaced by an eerie quietness – an unfamiliar sense of serenity. You could mistake it all for the blissful surroundings of a Spanish villa. All that's missing is a crystal-clear, turquoise-blue pool.

But, as I scan the beautiful environment, it isn't long until the disturbing sounds of modern warfare return.

'Lads on the roof!' Zach calls out. 'Keep an eye out for Terry. He's lost sight of us, but knows roughly where we are.'

'Terry' is a nickname adopted by all friendly forces for our enemy. On hearing Terry's name, the calm I felt is replaced with tension.

The ground I can see is a small piece of land – a hundred metres square, boxed off on all sides by tall trees and deep ditches. Little can be seen beyond it, with dark shadows making excellent cover for any prying eyes.

'Guys,' adds the interpreter, 'Terry watched our troop come into this village, but has lost sight of us.'

Tommo, a fellow marine, calls up. 'Stay frosty!' he jokes, mimicking the phrase from the global best-selling game *Call of Duty*.

Four of us watch the trees to our front, waiting for Terry to appear. And, on cue, part of the treeline rustles and a young male, maybe in his late teens, steps into the open. My jaw drops.

He's dressed all in black and wearing trainers – Terry's preferred choice of footwear. To his face, he's holding some form of equipment, possibly a radio. Is this the guy who the interpreter can hear on his own radio?

This young male seems oblivious to our presence. Looking around, yet lacking intent. Staring more at his feet than searching for a troop of marines. Is he untrained, shit, or distracted? We will soon find out.

'Zach. ZACH!' Gav shouts through whispers. 'Ask the interpreter if he can still hear the Taliban on his radio.'

A long few seconds pass as Zach checks. 'Yeah, he can. Why?'

'I think we've got eyes on him, mate,' Gav alerts. Every marine below now is readying themselves and getting to their feet.

My body goes cold and my heart races. I pull my weapon tight into my shoulder and lay my sights on the lone male. 'This guy is fucked,' I say to myself.

As taught in training, I enter my breathing cycle and slow myself down. Focusing now on accurately controlling even the most minimal movements of my weapon.

As I breathe in, my weapon slowly rises. As I breathe out, my weapon slowly lowers, my aim forever travelling up and down the unsuspecting male, head to toe.

'Fuck me, he's clueless. I can't believe he hasn't seen us yet,' whispers Bluey to my left.

No excitement in his voice, just concern. *Are we about to make the right call in killing him?* I can't help but think.

We all look through our sights, four heavily armed marines lying flat on the roof, with the drop on our enemy.

The young man's face is so clear, his innocent expression portraying a lost boy locked in a vicious environment; not a hardened warrior.

Is it his choice to be here? Is he being forced to use that radio – the Taliban's malicious recruiting strategies moulding another boy soldier?

But there's no time for questions or sympathy. If he's reporting on our location, then our lives are under threat, so we must react in defence – whatever that entails.

Still with the radio to his face, he begins walking down a small path towards our compound.

'Jesus Christ. He's walking straight towards us!' says Bluey. 'Shit, he's completely unaware!' adds Gav.

My eyes widen. He's no more than twenty metres from us, with four well-trained riflemen aiming at his chest. I can see everything about him, from the colour of his laces down to the pigmentation on his skin. This is close combat, and my god, do we have the upper hand!

I can't help but think about the images we will all soon witness. Within the next few seconds, gunfire will echo. And all four of us will watch another young enemy fighter drop and take his last few breaths as he slips away.

I take another deep breath and train my sights once more on his body. I switch my safety catch off, ready to fire, moving my index finger onto the trigger, my adrenaline flowing like a river.

Sweat makes my skin stick to the smooth metal I'm caressing. I add pressure and slowly depress it – my heart racing faster and faster. This is it, I'm going to kill this young Taliban. I take a last breath, holding it in as I prepare to shoot. *Here I go . . . there's no looking back now!*

But I don't pull the trigger. Not one of us fires.

An abrupt thought has frozen my desire to shoot.

Suddenly, something doesn't feel right. A nagging sensation releases my finger pressure from the trigger.

We aren't murderers. This boy may be Taliban, but he hasn't got a weapon. He's not an instant threat.

Instead of shooting him, we can detain him, question him, discover more from him than we would if he's face down, bleeding to death on the path.

'Fucking stop that guy!' Gav commands to those below, clearly thinking the same as me.

Several marines bomb-burst out of the compound and grab the young man as he wanders by. The fright in his eyes quickly indicates to us that this didn't add up at all.

My body's tension releases. I move to the edge of the compound roof to watch the boss, the interpreter and several marines tactically questioning the kid.

'It's a wind-up radio,' someone calls to us. 'He's listening to some shit music.'

Realizing how tense I must have been, my shoulders relax with relief and I rain curses. 'Tell him not to walk around looking like he's a member of the FUCKING Taliban, wandering around a fucking enemy hotspot on a pissing radio. Twat!'

My comments are harsh and angry, unsympathetic to the young boy's naivety. Yet the cursing also flows from sheer relief, thankful that we didn't release the shots that would have inevitably ended his innocent young life.

'They can see us now,' the interpreter calls back out. 'They say they can see four men lying on a roof, and report we have just taken someone in.'

'Fuck! This is relentless,' I say to the other three on the roof – Bluey, Gav and Jonesy. 'You can't win!'

Again, I tense and am back on full alert. Yet a strange feeling of relief creeps in. Though my entire body was pent-up, sweating and tightening with the fear of killing someone at such close range, my mental courage to do the right thing and take control of my body kicked in and avoided what would have been a horrific moment, saving the young man's life.

Afghanistan is psychologically intense – a stampede of diverse situations that constantly test your ability to think with clarity.

It isn't hard to pull the trigger without thinking clearly and make a mistake you would have to live with for ever.

Thank fuck we're trained to always THINK about doing the right thing, to always employ moral courage.

'Now, where the fuck is Terry?'

COURAGE

↑

INSPIRATION

6.
Get Out of Your Comfort Zone

LET'S MAKE FEAR WORK FOR US

For a Commando, many situations automatically induce feelings of dread, worry, doubt and anxiety: from sitting in the back of a Chinook hurtling towards an enemy battlefield, to being crammed together within the confines of a landing craft destined for an exposed beach-head. Adrenal responses activate and unwanted thoughts can quickly plague the mind.

What if I get shot running straight off the ramp? Am I going to tread on a hidden explosive? These are internal questions that can't be avoided. Every soldier faces them.

However, gaining control of ourselves, as quickly as we can, will free up our thinking, allowing us to concentrate on the mission at hand and make the right decisions. For example, when we were aiming at that young man we suspected to be part of the Taliban, we didn't get so carried away by our fear of the threat or possible danger that we made the wrong decision. In the end, we remained clear minded, faced our fear and then made the (right) decision not to pull the trigger.

You need to get used to facing your fear, feeling your fear, and then making it work for you. That way you can step out of your comfort zone and advance towards making your ambition come true.

STEPPING OUTSIDE YOUR COMFORT ZONE

Your comfort zone can be a bad, negative, habit-breeding place. It's the reason for much of your uninspired behaviour, holding you back from what you truly want, keeping you locked within a ring of safety. It is the psychological state in which things are familiar to you, where you feel at ease and in control of the environment you're in.

> Our comfort zone makes us overweight, unhealthy, bored, broke and tired. It creates unwilling attitudes towards doing things that may test us, preventing us from exploring the unknown and growing as a person.

Your comfort zone is as it describes itself – a place in which you feel comfortable and safe.

We all have one.

There's no shame in admitting what provides you with security. You may find there are things you will sprint out of your comfort zone for while others hold you back in its vice-like grip. Stepping out of your comfort zone can produce low levels of anxiety and stress, but it can also help you to thrive and grow.

—Pause for thought—

What does your comfort zone look like? What makes you feel safe? What makes you feel uncomfortable?

In which areas of your life do you dare strive towards the unknown and which are too scary?

What goals are you confident you will complete and which ones cause concern?

Consider the inspirations that have led to your newfound goals. Are any of them the reasons why you stay within your comfort zone?

Although they drive your passion and you have a burning desire to complete them, do any of your goals induce fear and panic?

MOVING UP AND OUT OF YOUR COMFORT ZONE

When you move towards the boundaries of your comfort zone, you will not only face your fears in a positive way but also learn and grow a great deal. Instead of picturing the spaces inside and outside your comfort zone as two distinct areas, try to think of the stages you pass through if you leave it and what you overcome and learn as you move further from it. The diagram illustrates the journey of discovery you go on when

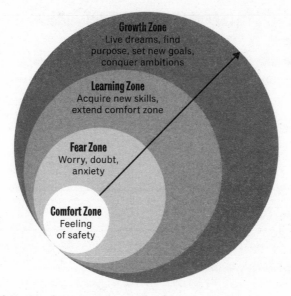

The journey from comfort zone to growth zone.

you push through your comfort zone, past the fear zone, into the learning zone, where you acquire new skills, and then into the growth zone, where you find purpose, conquer ambitions and learn about yourself on a deeper level. Pushing past your comfort zone into the unknown doesn't have to be a scary thing – look at all you stand to gain. Pushing beyond the limiting world of your comfort zone exposes you to situations you would rarely face, forcing you to think and behave differently in order to succeed, and thus learn more about yourself and the world.

> Expanding your experiences outside your comfort zone can build your confidence and self-esteem, and help you to be more creative. It also forces you to learn about yourself, encourages you to overcome challenges, and will bring new rewards.

Tackling the unknown, you prove to yourself that you can push past your boundaries and limiting beliefs. Insecurity loves to feed on the negative habits of not trying, but exhibiting courage and pushing yourself through effort will feed confidence.

FOUR STEPS TO LEAVING YOUR COMFORT ZONE

In order to move away from what you find comfortable and into the realms of growth you're going to need a strategy.

The following strategy features a few specific areas I feel you should concentrate on if you intend to move beyond what you feel comfortable with.

STEP ONE – Identify the boundaries of your comfort zone

Reflections & Actions	Questions
Think hard about what holds you back from your goals.	Why haven't you achieved these goals yet?
From your journal, pick out those goals you feel you've put off up until this point in life.	Why have you not felt comfortable enough up to this point to complete them?

Ask yourself the questions opposite.	Why do these goals, and not your other ones, seem more difficult?
	Why is now suddenly the right time?
	What are the feelings and sensations you encounter when you think of these goals?
	What is it that has denied you success up to this point?
	What are you going to do about it?

When you're approaching the edge of your comfort zone, when you begin to engage in a task, you will begin to feel the adrenal and neural effects we discussed in Chapter 5.

Thinking about the goals you're questioning above, do they induce the adrenal feelings you associate with fear? The effects that increase your heart rate and release butterflies in your stomach? If they do, you're in a good place. They're highlighting to you that you're identifying your boundaries of comfort, stepping away from your comfort zone. If they don't induce these feelings, then they're goals that align only with comfort.

STEP TWO – Be specific about what you're overcoming

Reflections & Actions	Questions
Consider a time when you felt uncomfortable doing something new or that you didn't want to do but knew you should. It could be asking a stranger to be your mentor or delivering a presentation.	What exactly was it that was making you feel uncomfortable? Was it fear of being made to look stupid? Was it fear of failing? Was it fear of another person's response?
When you know what fear it was you were shying away from, ask yourself why.	Why was I scared of failing? Was it that I thought that meant I was worthless?
	Why was I afraid of what other people will think? Do I care about what they think?

For some, it may be difficult to identify whether these effects are induced by fear or excitement, as they can often be misinterpreted and confused with each other. Yet feeling them is the best sign you can have, as they let you know you're moving away from your comfort zone.

If you want to succeed, you must be specific about what keeps you in your comfort zone.

The ICE model is designed to ensure you know exactly what you want, before you go and get it. It's why we focused earlier on identifying meaningful and passionate inspirations. Then looked at transforming inspirations into focused goals in your life.

When times get tough and fear kicks in, your specific inspirations will be most valuable. Without them, you'll struggle to see through the challenge.

Instead of turning back in the face of fear, remember your inspiration. Let that inspiration drive you through your comfort zone, and be really specific about what it is that is stopping you leaving it.

STEP THREE – Leave your comfort zone slowly

Reflections & Actions	Questions
When moving towards something unfamiliar, think about doing it gradually.	Next time you face moving out of your comfort zone, ask yourself, 'What's the smallest step I can handle right now?'
Allow yourself to get used to being outside your comfort zone one step at a time, don't plunge yourself entirely into the discomfort zone all in one go.	

If your goal was to be the fastest person ever to swim the English Channel, you wouldn't just get changed and dive straight in. You'd train first in the pool, then in a lake, then in the sea, until you were ready for the challenge. Jumping in and trying to do it straightaway would almost certainly result in failure – failure you'd perceive as final, shutting down your ambition.

STEP FOUR – Adjust your daily routine

Reflections & Actions	Questions
Courage begins by doing what you don't want to do.	Are you more inclined to come home from work and put your feet up with a takeaway than go out for a run?
Begin introducing doses of discomfort and fear into your daily routine.	How are you really going to complete the marathon you've made your lifelong goal?
	What can you do to stop yourself from taking the easy route? Can you put your trainers by the end of your bed in the morning or at your front door so when you wake up or come home from work you've created a new habit?

Your daily routine underpins much of your comfort zone. Without you realizing, it determines the likelihood of completing your most ambitious goals.

Your daily 'feet up' routine is breeding poor habits that will hold you in your comfort zone and have a catastrophic impact on the success you want. Whether your goal is to run a marathon, learn a new language or deliver a public speech by the end of the year, you have to take yourself out of your comfort zone towards that goal every day in small ways.

A Commando doesn't necessarily want to make the desperate sprint through a hail of gunfire to reach the shelter of the next building. Nor does he want to wake up at four in the morning, mid-January, to go on guard during a training exercise. But he will, because he knows he must.

You don't necessarily want to go for a run in the rain, but you know you must. You might not want to have that difficult discussion with someone, but you know you must. Your courage starts with this same approach – facing something you don't want to do and doing it anyway.

A good way of making sure you change your daily habit is to

employ what author and motivational speaker Mel Robbins calls the 5-second rule. Robbins devised a way to help procrastinators get off their arse and complete a task – *before* they convince themselves not to do it.

In her book *The 5 Second Rule*, Mel encourages the reader to take five seconds to snap out of that negative 'I can't be bothered' thinking and into action. You simply count down from five. She insists that, if you can make even the slightest movement towards the task or goal before you get down to one, you will succeed. So, if you're deliberating whether to go for that run, do another hour of studying or choose the unhealthy food option, count down to five and start walking to your trainers, walk towards your laptop or close the Just Eat page.

To own the Commando mindset and make it applicable to your life, you must learn to avoid becoming a procrastinator. You are swiftly going to take yourself to the next level, simply by embracing what you don't want to do.

THREE QUESTIONS TO STRENGTHEN YOUR RESOLVE

Accomplishing any dream or goal can be tough, but the difference between failure and success is mental preparation. When people don't achieve something it's less to do with the challenge or task than their mindset. Some people over-think success before even committing to action. They make countless plans and strategies but never do anything towards achieving them. Conversely, some people under-think it. They don't consider sufficiently how they are going to achieve something or the methods and support they need to do it.

You need to find the midpoint between over- and under-thinking to make sure you achieve your ambitions. The next three questions are designed to help spur you on – they'll encourage you to find the right balance between thinking and acting.

Have you identified your self-imposed limits yet?

Read the following sentence and digest it as fast as you can:

> You are the ONLY reason for your lack of success – not the situation or anyone else around you!

Does that statement cause offence, or awareness?

Do you get defensive, or do you go on the attack for success?

You are the only person who controls your destiny. If your perception of my comment is negative, you may be acting with a fixed mindset rather than a growth mindset and have imposed limits on yourself.

Your inability to accept that it is *your fault* – and no one else's – is what is holding you back. You're not taking accountability for your own destiny.

Consider the following questions:

- Do you often find yourself saying, 'I can't'?
- Do you look to others for approval?
- Are the people around you negative?
- Do you allow people to offend you and hurt you emotionally?
- Are you controlled by what you think?
- Is your thinking often negative? If so, can you identify the impact it has on you?

If you have answered yes to any of these questions, you have immediately identified one or more self-imposed limitations.

A self-imposed limitation is something attributed only by yourself, where *you* become the root cause. It doesn't necessarily stem from what you say to yourself or how you allow situations and people around you to dictate your decisions. It can also be influenced by how hard a task you set yourself and the expectations that entails.

For example, if you find yourself disappointed at not completing your daily to-do list, have you considered the possibility that you set yourself too many tasks?

Does the thought of 'biting off more than you can chew' spring to mind if you find yourself regularly failing to achieve small goals? This is also self-imposed. Try considering how much you're setting yourself and whether what you set is achievable. If you don't, you might find yourself failing and then failing again.

Do you view fear as a signpost to success?

When a challenge daunts you and those neural and hormonal responses trigger, that's when you know you're making progress. Success rarely comes easily, otherwise nothing would be worth anything.

When those 'combat indicators' of fear kick in – sweating, heart rate, breathing, muscular tension – you are doing something right. You're edging towards success.

Look at the zonal image again. The first circle is the comfort zone; the second is where fear arises; the third and fourth are where you learn and grow.

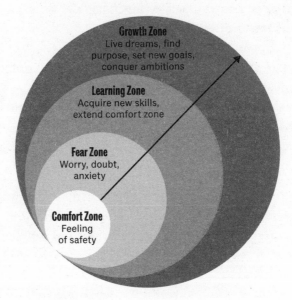

In relation to this image, consider the following scenario:

You are stuck on a very small desert island with only caught fish to eat and trapped rainwater to drink – if it rains. You've made a *small bivouac for shelter and happily created fire. Life is **OK**, you will likely survive, just alone and bored. However, merely 1,000 metres away, you can see land with civilization – a more appealing place to survive. Between you and the land is calm, open, swimmable water, but you think there may be sharks in it. If you stay on your island, you'll have to endure a lifetime of fish, loneliness and bore-dom. If you get to the new land, you will be rewarded with a far more fulfilling and enjoyable life. What do you do?*

Of course, you'll attempt swimming to the new island! It's only a kilo-metre. And, though sharks may be out there, you haven't seen any.

I know it's a far-fetched example. You're probably thinking more about Tom Hanks in *Castaway* than overcoming fear. However, this is how I want you to imagine life when you consider stepping out of your comfort zone.

Your comfort zone (the first circle) is routine and mundane, but it is survivable. Yet, the new island (circles three and four) offers a more fulfilling and prosperous life. All you need to do is get there – you must have the courage to take the risk of swimming with the sharks (circle two).

Look at your life so far. Many things you've done to date will have required you to push through some form of fear boundary. You'll often have had to commit to actions over the years that have induced fear. Yet, without pushing through, you'd never have made it to where you are now. Even simply crossing a busy road to get to the other side is like overcoming the (possibly) shark-infested water.

Fear is a signpost that you are heading in the right direction, that you are making headway to the more prosperous island. Acknowledge the fear, but swim through it.

Did you know you'll grow?

Are you wondering whether, after the second island, there might be another bigger, more fulfilling one? And what about the island after that?

Every time you want to swim to the next bigger and better island, you will ultimately have to face your fears again of swimming with the sharks.

In psychologist Susan Jeffers's book *Feel the Fear and Do It Anyway*, she talks about *expanding* your comfort zone. There are several hurdles of risk you must overcome in order to expand it, the idea being that the more you expose yourself to fear and risk, the more your comfort zone expands as you become more accustomed to difficulty and challenge.

You may be thinking, *I thought I was trying to escape my comfort zone, not expand it?*

When you begin to take on and challenge your fears, you're not only trying to overcome what may scare you, you're also beginning to grow your ability and potential.

Take, for example, your current job. Go back to your first days in the position. No matter what it is, as well as being excited you'll have probably spent your first day or so being nervous, unsure, and a little daunted by what you had to do. You didn't know any other staff members and were over-polite to everyone you met, just in case they were in a position of importance. And you did your utmost to get everything right, to avoid looking stupid on your first day. Now think how you feel when you go to work today. Are you in that same state of fear and worry or do you feel comfortable?

That first day, you were way outside your comfort zone; today, you're well inside it. You've increased your confidence, understanding and skill. All this is a result of expanding your comfort zone. If and when promotion comes, you'll again feel the pressure of the unknown. Once more, you'll have to leave your comfort zone. And so on.

Everyone must start somewhere, before they can grow and develop into more than they were. Professional athletes, musicians, entrepreneurs, politicians, movie stars and the like were all nervous and worried on their first day, just as you were, before they grew into the confident and acclaimed people we see today.

YOU CAN'T FAIL IF YOU'RE STILL IN THE GAME

You will never fail if you stick with it and stay in the game – never, ever quitting. You *will* encounter setbacks and losses, and be unsuccessful at moments throughout your journey, but, while these are inevitable, remember failure is not.

In this context, failure and failing are two different things. A short-term failing isn't an overall failure, it's a lesson that will educate you about what you need to do better the next time. These mini-failings allow you to reassess and take action, putting everything you've learned into your next move.

If a marine scores low on a shooting test, it isn't a failure; rather, it teaches them to go away and practise harder and hone their skills. They don't stop being a marine.

When a football team lose, they don't give up and exit the league. They learn from their mistakes and analyses, get fitter, train harder and go again. When someone fails an exam, they don't give up, they study harder and resit the test. If a candidate doesn't win an election, they don't give up, they stand again.

No matter how many setbacks you face, if you stay in the game you will eventually succeed.

Every time you step from your comfort zone, you are unlocking new potential and you are growing. Even if it doesn't turn out how you wanted it to, at least you have tried and can rethink your strategy, then go again. This is what those with an ambitious Commando mindset do. Constantly strive for more and never, ever give up!

From this point onwards, there are no longer any excuses for you to use against yourself. You are the one in control. You are the only one who can make the decision to step from the realms of your comfort zone or stay locked within its confines.

Will you dare swim with the sharks?

Commando Mindset is all about harnessing what challenges you and turning it into strengths. You need to assess everything that causes you to be scared, anxious or worried and question how it can make you stronger, not weaker.

As you move through the rest of the book, keep your fears in the forefront of your mind. Take every opportunity you get to challenge yourself – even if it has nothing to do with your goals. Constantly step outside your comfort zone and force yourself to do things the old you would never have done. Demonstrate to yourself your capabilities and strengths.

With every single step you dare take, your positivity and confidence, courage and belief will grow ever stronger.

BE READY FOR THE WALL

Energized? Feeling good? You should be. You should now have spent a considerable amount of time identifying your inspirations, thinking about how to translate them into goals and devising a strategy or plan to make sure you meet them.

By now, you should have a clear idea which of your ambitions are right for you to work on. You should be feeling confident and believe in yourself, ready to take the inspirations and big goals you have picked and translate them into manageable steps.

Is there a more motivating feeling than the light bulb pinging in your head now that you've determined what you want? I don't think there is, but it's also true that this feeling can fade quite quickly if you let doubts and fear creep in. Be conscious that this excited feeling may fade after the first few days or weeks.

Don't be afraid of re-energizing yourself with your journal. Look back on your achievements and remind yourself how far you have come. Reward yourself with a psychological boost drawn from previous achievements, ones you may have forgotten.

More and more of us are driven by instant gratification and, if we don't get what we want quickly, we swiftly move on to the next thing. But that's the average response and you're not average!

Midway through Commando training, recruits must endure and pass the bottom field assault course.

Those who fail either move backwards in training or leave Commando training completely.

You're wearing full combat fatigues and boots, 9.5kg of kit and a 5kg rifle.

Each recruit must effectively execute a vertical 12m rope climb and one lap of the assault course in under five minutes.

Oh, and a 200m fireman's carry of a partner wearing the same kit as them.

And a regain over a freezing water tank – a technique where you swing from a horizontal rope, before climbing back up, gripping on with your feet, then pulling yourself the rest of the way without falling in.

One of the obstacles on the assault course is the wall.

A brick wall similar to one you would find in your garden.

Two metres high.

Recruits must sprint at it and pull themselves up.

Then, all while keeping low to the top, you drop the other side and continue the course.

When carrying an extra 15kg and already exhausted, the wall seems to grow taller.

If you want to succeed and move on to the next phase of training, you must invest everything into getting over the wall.

You must run as fast as your legs will take you.

You must leap as high as you can.

You must endure the pain.

As your body crashes into the impenetrable structure, you must pull with all your might and determination.

And get over.

Every marine must overcome the wall.

And so must you.

Whatever you choose as your goals, you will at some point hit your own wall. Whether it's a physical or mental task, something will stand in your way and encourage failure. It will bully you with doubt and worry, trying its best to overwhelm you with fear.

You may be days, months or even years away from facing your wall, but it will undoubtedly come. So, the more ready you are, the better prepared you will be to face it.

Apprehension and fear, anxiety and doubt may creep in, but you are still clear in your mind what you want. You're driven by the knowledge that, on the other side of each challenge, wait natural neurological rewards: endorphins and dopamine, serotonin and oxytocin.

Anyone who adopts a Commando mindset is expecting the wall, ready for whatever challenge or adversity will be thrown his or her way, primed to overcome any obstacle. Having the plan is only half the battle. Being able to execute it, especially during times of doubt and struggle, is where your Commando mindset will shine through. None of your desires will ever come to fruition if you do not dare to take the physical leap of doing. For that, you will require courage.

ICE reflection 6:
Daily fears

As with ICE reflection 5, you're going to be facing some more fears, but this time alone.

You need to prove to yourself that you have the ability to push yourself when others aren't looking. It's time to embrace this challenge.

On a fresh page in your journal, write the heading 'A Week of Fear'. Under that, write 'Day One'.

As Eleanor Roosevelt famously said, 'You must do the thing

you think you cannot do.' For the next seven days, you're going to do exactly that.

Each day, pick something discomforting that induces your fears and face them. Be sensible about this; don't put yourself at risk of injury. Instead, try to overcome more everyday fears such as the ones you discovered earlier in the book.

Record each day what you chose to do and how it made you feel. Pinpoint the pleasure chemical rewards you think you received.

Do this and you'll be spending the next month expanding your comfort zone, forcing you to grow your courage, confidence and belief. This will prime you for the final stage of the Commando mindset: Enactment.

If you want to, you can include someone else in this challenge and you could hold each other to account, exchanging texts every day to let them know you've done something that scared you.

Commando tests

Here I am, standing at the starting line of the 'thirty-miler', the infamous fourth and final Commando test.

I see myself stepping foot off the train at the Commando training centre for the first time. Dressed in a cheap, poorly pressed suit, clutching a tightly packed holdall.

Since that moment, everything has moved at a hundred miles an hour.

As a troop, we have completed and passed the endurance course – three kilometres of submerged tunnels, hills, mud and water, followed by a six-kilometre run and a shooting test.

Also, the 15k or 'nine-miler' speed march – ninety minutes of repeatedly pounding your feet on hill roads, before finishing back at camp, drummed in by a lone member of the Royal Marines band.

The third test is the Tarzan assault course – a high-obstacle course beginning with a 20m death slide, followed by numerous 10m-high obstacles and ropes – that must be completed in under thirteen minutes.

The Commando tests are both physically and mentally demanding. After months of the world's hardest infantry training, my legs are heavy, arms tired. Physical exhaustion is swiftly creeping in.

Each test is conducted with you carrying 9.5kg of weight in your webbing plus a 5kg rifle, wearing heavy boots and combat fatigues. Chafing, sores, stiffness and blisters are rife, forcing the mental toughness to kick in.

Now, today, here we all stand. At the beginning of one of the most revered military tests in the world – thirty miles between us and success.

Throughout the British military, this route is one of the hardest tests outside Special Forces selection. It's synonymous with becoming a Commando, claiming fame throughout history as a path many legends have trodden. Dartmoor National Park is its home, a landscape that brings many challenges of its own.

Cruel moors, weather and terrain. Eight months of exhausting training. Heavy kit, tired bodies and fractured minds. There's good reason why the thirty-miler has such a fearsome reputation.

But at this moment, determination, adrenaline and trepidation are filling me with drive. In eight hours, hopefully I'll lay hands upon my own green beret.

However, thirty miles stand between me and my new place within Britain's elite – it will take immense courage to push to the very end.

In a perfect scenario, I'd start a challenge like this well rested and recuperated. But that's not the way of Commando training, which is specifically designed to ensure you can overcome the most testing challenges when your body is on the brink of exhaustion.

We step off, into the dark of night, with dawn yet to break.

Within minutes, we're climbing the first hill, the sharp incline reminding every muscle in our bodies that they are fucked.

Though I start cold, in just a shirt, I'm soon thankful it's the only layer I'm wearing as my body begins to warm up.

For the next hour, we cross flooded bogs and relentless terrain. Then dawn breaks to reveal a blanket of grey fog, engulfing the ground ahead. Only the next fifty metres are visible. After that, mere guesswork.

Eight miles in, we arrive at the dreaded rollercoaster – several sharp hills that follow one after the other, so steep I clutch at tufts of grass to pull myself up. I'm hurting. Every step drains me further. Every part of me is saying 'Stop!'

Yet, when I look around, almost all the lads in my section seem composed and resilient, fuelling me to rustle up more courage and join them in their look of strength.

'Dig deep, lads, almost a third of the route done,' my corporal calls out.

A third! I think to myself. *Feels like we've been going for fucking ages.*

I'm resisting the urge to ask, 'Are we nearly there yet?' Avoiding the embarrassment of acting like a petulant child in the back seat on a long journey.

At the halfway point, soggy warm pasties greet us. Though looking very unappealing, it's by far one of the nicest things I've ever eaten.

It's a cold day on the open moorland. As soon as we stop, the bitter wind attacks my sweat-soaked clothing, sending chills through my body. The pasty's warmth is extremely welcome.

Water bottles topped up, stomachs full, we press on. Five hours have now passed since we left Okehampton battle camp at the far north of Dartmoor. We're nearing almost two-thirds of the route complete.

Though my body is tired, and every single bit of kit is rubbing and chafing, for the first time on the march I feel strong.

Unfortunately, along the way, we've lost several guys who couldn't keep up with the pack or fell to injury. The majority of us remaining all take a bit of comfort in not being among the ones who dropped out.

We press on, seven hours in the bag, upwards of twenty-five miles complete. Now that the green beret is almost within touching distance, the route grows rapidly harder. My legs feel like rusty joints. Lower back is stiff and tight. Shoulders ache from the weight of my kit. And I'm growing tired of only being able to see the next fifty metres ahead.

But this is where the thirty-miler wants me to get off.

This is where the revered test is about to challenge every single one of us to the core.

I'm so tantalizingly close to success, yet feel so far away. The negative parts of my mind pray to stop, give up, chuck it in. My mental wall is inbound.

I know, deep within, this is why the Royal Marines use this test at the very end of training – to expose every one of us to our true selves.

If you can fight through the mental blockade that waits ahead in the next few miles, you should be able to overcome any challenge you face in the future.

'Here it comes!' I mutter to myself. Body drained. Nothing left. On the ropes. 'Just give up and do it next week in another troop!'

My irrational voice is talking to me, looking for the control of my legs. It's mile twenty-six and part of me wants to wrap.* I need to battle this. I need to overcome this way of feeling and reiterate to myself again and again that I am capable, we are all capable, of achieving this.

I tell the irrational voice to fuck off.

* Give up.

Think about everything you've overcome, Ben.

Your parents' divorce. School bullies.

Witnessing a nightclubber's death. Drink and drugs.

Suicidal thoughts. The doubters and naysayers who said you'd never get to this point – the point they never had the courage to get to themselves. And think about the many previous months of training before today.

Looking around, I realize I'm surrounded by utter excellence, men of all ages digging equally deep as I am. This fuels me with courage. I'm four miles from the end and about to smash through my wall. I want to be by these lads alongside me right now.

With gritted teeth, I pluck up the last ounce of energy I own and fucking go for it. This is what the Royal Marines want to see from me. This is what it means to be a Royal Marines Commando – courage and determination in the face of extreme hardship.

Eight hours in, we sail over the small humpback bridge that crosses a thin river in the heart of Dartmoor. We have passed the fourth Commando test. We have passed Royal Marines training.

As the soft cloth of the green beret touches my cold hands, I mould my hard-earned prize to my head. I look back at my remaining troop who, too, all proudly wear their own green beret.

It isn't about what the cloth on our head is, it's about what it means and represents, how much it takes to achieve it and, even more, to retain it.

'Williams!' says my corporal. 'Fucking good effort!' He shakes my hand. To have gained the respect and praise of my instructors – who for so long seem to have hated us all – means the world.

'Welcome to the club, Royal!' he finishes, before walking away.

Only Royal Marines Commandos call each other 'Royal'. Up to this point, I've merely answered to a shouted 'Oi!' or 'Recruit!'

I try to make my exterior look steely.

Yet, inside, I'm jumping around like the excited young boy who once stood in the Royal Marines museum so many years ago.

COURAGE

↑

INSPIRATION

7.
Believe in Yourself

TO OWN COURAGE, YOU MUST HAVE BELIEF

Aside from getting clean, Commando training is by far the toughest thing I've ever done – although being a father to a young boy and girl comes extremely close.

The physical and mental challenges, the continuous pressure, regularly experiencing the fears of injury or failure collectively burden the mind. The standards are so extremely high. If you don't reach them, you are swiftly shown the door.

Courage got me through. Courage based on the long-held belief that I was going to be a Royal Marines Commando. Today, I introduce what I have learned in the Royal Marines to other people who are striving for success in their own different ways.

Antony and I recently delivered the Finding Your Edge workshop to Wasps RFC. Working with the Premiership rugby club's academy provided an opportunity to test the young players' belief.

Life can be very competitive in professional sports academies, as all of the young and talented players are fighting for a contract at the end of their trial. Of the thirty or so players with whom we ran the workshop, it's likely only a handful – maybe two or three – will be selected for a professional career.

Halfway through our workshop I posed a question: 'Who here believes they will make it as a professional rugby player?'

Less than 50 per cent of the players put their hands up.

Among a group of people you'd expect to have implicit belief in themselves, this was a concerning statistic. I looked around, wondering about who I thought would and would not make it as a professional. I was pretty sure it would be those who said they believed in themselves.

Apply yourself

A week later, I was sitting down with a good friend – Pete Kelly, CEO of Imployable, a company that makes a tech-based recruitment app.

I was telling Pete about the rugby academy players not having enough belief. 'I don't know how people can be like that!' was his reply. 'When I started Imployable, I had every belief that it would work.'

Pete and his team started their company from scratch. Within a year they were valued at £3.3 million, featured in the American business magazine *Forbes*, breaking records and receiving numerous awards and accolades. Pretty impressive for a former Royal Marine who was once in substantial debt and unemployed after his military career.

'Even though at times I knew I was way over my head – with a bit of cloak and dagger, I knew I could make it work,' Pete added. 'I had to make it work. Things don't happen half-heartedly, they happen when every single part of you knows it will happen, even if fear is looming at the back of your head.'

Pete is right. He's come from nothing – orphaned, broke and unemployed – to becoming a Commando, before founding the groundbreaking Imployable app. His business is partnered with Google. Clients include the likes of BP, the Department of Justice and Renault's racing division. It's all down to how much he applied himself and believed in himself, especially during periods of uncertainty.

'The doubt, worry and fear were always there, but I knew I could do it,' Pete insisted.

'I'm glad I own a Commando mindset. This is where my belief is driven from.'

—Pause for thought—

Wherever you are, put the book down for a minute. If you're out in a public space, great. If not, use your imagination. I want you to open your eyes to the world. Watch the people around you or passing by. Pick a few out at random and imagine what belief they have used to get to where they are.

- Can you spot the mother who has had to build up great courage to get through childbirth?
- How has that policeman gained the immense belief to keep doing what he does every day?
- The owner of the shop over there, how has she built up her belief to get her business to where it's at?
- What about the young man with an armful of textbooks? Does he own the belief to get through his exam?
- That finance director completing her PowerPoint presentation in a coffee shop on a weekend. Does she have sufficient confidence to deliver an important talk on the company's financial situation?

When you are done people watching, consider your own belief and how it has or has not affected your own life. Are you someone who 'fakes it until you make it'? Or are you someone who truly believes in yourself?

Belief is the backbone of courage

See it anywhere you look. Every day, in all walks of life, people are believing in themselves so deeply they find the inner ability to push themselves far outside their comfort zones, knowing that it will benefit them.

The Wasps academy players I delivered the workshop to are all extremely fit, highly skilled and very talented. Physically, every single one of them has the potential to make the grade and win a contract. However, if a player is lacking the mental belief that they can actually achieve a contract, it is highly likely they won't.

Back when I was instructing Royal Marines recruits myself at the Commando training centre, I would often witness so many young and talented men falling by the wayside because they simply no longer believed in themselves. When things got mentally and physically demanding, their belief would wane and they would pull out of training.

— Exercise: Your belief —

Belief is what binds your courage, the power of knowing for certain that you will persevere towards success.

- Identify an occasion where you lacked belief and failed at what you were trying to do.
- Think of a time where your belief was so strong, it gave you the power and determination to succeed.

THE POWER OF SELF-BELIEF

It may sound surprising to you, but one of my biggest inspirations in life who portrayed immense self-belief is author J. K. Rowling. Her tale of coming from nothing to achieve extraordinary things is something beyond incredible.

When I was starting out on my own writing journey back in 2016, I had no sign of an agent, and with that, very little hope of a book deal. Tapping away on an old laptop in a cramped cupboard under the stairs (not unlike the one Harry Potter lived in!), I would rise at 4 a.m. to write before anyone woke up, cramming in a few hours before work. Then I would continue writing late into the night after a day as a Royal Marines instructor.

After a year of writing, I submitted my proposal to almost a hundred agents and waited patiently. *No, not for us,* one email returned. *There isn't a market for this at the moment,* another read. *We don't feel your writing is strong enough. We aren't sure you carry enough credibility in this field,* came a final blow. Out of the ninety-six agents I emailed, only thirteen bothered to reply, and only one was willing to take me on as a client.

I am thankful to have met my first agent, but unfortunately it didn't turn out the way I expected. She introduced me to several major publishers, all of whom were happy to hear my pitch, but none of whom wanted to take my book any further. I soon realized that my agent had bought into my character rather than my book, and so we parted ways. I had hit a wall and slumped like a failure.

When I first came across J. K. Rowling's story of success, I was struck by her drive. Harry Potter made his way into her head while she sat on a delayed train from Manchester to London. For the next five years, she began piecing together *Harry Potter and the Philosopher's Stone.*

Rowling's mother died before she was able to share the idea of Harry with her, and she went on a downward spiral of depression as regrets for that whirled around her head. Confused, Rowling embarked on a new life in Portugal teaching English, where she met her husband and gave birth to her daughter in 1993.

But the marriage ended swiftly, and within a few months of her daughter's birth she returned to Edinburgh, no further forward than when she left. Though she has described that as the time when she reached rock bottom, she also said at a speech she delivered at a Harvard graduation in 2008:

'I was set free, because my greatest fear had been realized, and I was still alive, and I still had a daughter whom I adored, an old typewriter and a big idea. And so rock bottom became the solid foundation on which I rebuilt my life.'

Believing deeply in herself, she began to approach literary agents, succeeding at her third attempt. The next hurdle was to find a publisher. Her first rejection note was followed by another, then another. Ten more rejection slips later, she was still sending proposals out with belief, before the book was accepted by Bloomsbury. The rest is history.

Rowling's self-belief and determination spurred me on. Even when she was at rock bottom, she never lost hope; she kept driving, epitomizing everything I believe the Commando mindset ought to be.

She *knew* Harry Potter was going to succeed, and that drove her belief so deeply that every setback was just another reason to keep going. She exemplified self-belief.

I always knew *Commando Mindset* could be worth publishing, and J. K. Rowling's inspiring story of tenacity and self-belief reminded me of that when I needed it most. Her own path guided me back to the PC, and to revisit my own book's proposal. You probably wouldn't be reading this now had I never been inspired by J. K. Rowling's own story.

MIND HOW YOU SPEAK TO YOURSELF

Sometimes, belief can fade or diminish, if only for a slight moment. And it's at that point you must bring forward into your consciousness what you are thinking. Just take the sentiment *I can't*, for example:

What does *I can't* mean to you? To me it means one or more, and usually all, of the following:

- *I won't.*
- *I'm not going to.*
- *I can't be bothered.*

- *I'm lazy.*
- *I lack belief.*

How you speak about your approach towards challenge and difficulty will itself affect your subsequent behaviour.

If you find yourself always saying 'I can't,' are you really likely to succeed?
All you are saying is 'I won't,' just in a different way.
To grow your belief, you must change your vocabulary.

— Pause for thought —

Look at the examples below and identify how drastic an effect the *I can't* phrase can have on your success.

I can't do this job = I won't do this job. You can establish the resources, knowledge and skills to help you excel at your job. *I can't* means you won't or can't be bothered to.

I can't quit my job and start a business = I won't quit my job and start a business. It takes courage to quit and even more courage to start a business. But *I can't* is the excuse that will stop it all from happening.

I can't stop smoking = I won't stop smoking. Anyone can do it, it's whether you own the desire, determination and resilience to quit that makes the difference.

I can't train today = I won't train today. Unless injury or illness is holding you back, you can train. You might just need to get up earlier or reorganize your day to fit it in.

Stop telling yourself you can't do something. If it's not something you want to do right now, that's OK. Own up to the fact that whatever it is isn't your priority right now rather than pretending to yourself you can't do it for one reason or another. It limits you and makes you doubt your self-belief.

Removing the phrase *I can't* from your sentences will immediately encourage positivity, determination and courage. It will
fuel belief.

SURROUND YOURSELF WITH EXCELLENCE

It's common knowledge that you become the people you surround
yourself with, and that the environment you create has an enormous
impact on whether you're successful or not.

What is your environment?
Who are you currently surrounded by?
How positive are they?
Are they driven?
Do they own the same desire for success as you do?

Consider the last two questions. If you answered yes to both, then
brilliant. But if you answered no, you must stop and think whether they
are the right people to be around.

Surround yourself with excellence and you'll become excellent.
Surround yourself with negativity, people who are content to live in
their comfort zone and with no self-belief, and you will naturally start
to think this way too.

According to American entrepreneur, motivational speaker and
author Jim Rohn, 'You are the average of the five people you spend
the most time with.' For some, that figure may be more than five; for
others, fewer. Yet the message is clear – you are most likely to become
like those you surround yourself with.

Want to be a millionaire? Then hang out with millionaires.

Want to be a good parent? Then hang out with good parents.

Want to be the best in your field? Then surround yourself with
the best.

—Pause for thought—

- Are you susceptible to a sneaky cigarette when offered by a friend, even though you hate the taste?
- Have you ever found yourself saying yes to a night out, when instead you knew you should have stayed in to save money?
- Have you been around people who have made a wrong decision, but you kept quiet in fear of being judged?
- Have you not followed through on something you desire, because those you associate with are moving in a different direction, or don't agree with your goals?
- Do you allow others to make decisions for you?

STAY TRUE TO YOURSELF

More than likely, you have given a mixture of positive and negative answers to the questions in the 'Pause for thought' box above. Either way, be honest with yourself about how impressionable you might be and how often your let you own beliefs be influenced by others.

Consider the environment and people you spend most time with – could they be holding you back? Conforming takes far less effort than going against the grain, but can be detrimental to your belief and courage.

I'm privileged to have been part of a military community made up of highly motivated and driven people. We lived and trained together, spending more time with each other than with our own families. I was always surrounded by inspiring individuals, people who helped me become who I am today. I lived alongside people who were like minded. In them, I recognized the calibre of person who drew out the best from me and helped increase my courage and self-belief.

Though you may struggle to live and breathe a life with those you'd most like to surround yourself with, the opportunity to grow in the excellence and presence of others is still vast.

Networking opportunities occur in hotel lobbies almost every morning in every city and town. Experts run regular seminars up and down the country to share how they achieved success. And there are thousands of forums and social-media groups – with millions of members – for people who want to grow, raise the bar on their personal development and achieve their ambitions.

The world we live in is so technically advanced that everything and everyone is there for us at our fingertips. Smartphones, social media and global influencers have made it much easier to gain advice and help, training and coaching. These tools and methods are provided not only by people who are experts in their fields, but also often by individuals who have needed help themselves to walk the walk you want to walk yourself. If you're looking to surround yourself with new people and ideas more aligned with what you want today, you don't need to look far.

WHO SURROUNDS YOU ONLINE?

In the last couple of decades, social media has sonic boomed into society to become the most viewed and used platform in the world. Instagram, Twitter, Facebook, YouTube, Pinterest et al. are eating up hours of everyone's time and attention every day. We are addicted to checking our phones repeatedly for likes and comments, retweets and shares. Heck, I just pick up my phone and stare at the lock screen, purely out of habit. I don't even unlock it, I just look at it.

Technology and social media have become ingrained in our lives, with many of us practically addicted to the pleasurable feelings the gratification of likes and notifications elicit.

While I believe that most platforms are genuinely positive, I also feel social media has diverted us away from who we truly are. For many, it has subdued our inner courage to be who we really want to be. *If we actually did that, would the world like it? Would I be judged?*

While connecting billions of people around the world, social media can also divert our attention away from the realities of life. We see so many videos and pictures of people by a pool, looking out the window of a private jet, counting money, lifting weights and flaunting their bodies, that it becomes difficult to differentiate between real and fake.

As such, I encourage you to consider *who* you follow online, *what* they are posting, and *how* what they do influences your own decisions.

Social media 'friendship'

How many of the people you call 'friends' on Facebook, for example, would you actually stop and say hello to in the street?

How many are true friends that you could actually pick the phone up and call?

How many of them do you even own a number for?

And what about the people you follow on Instagram?

Do you follow them because of how they look, what they say, or what they do?

Do you follow them because everyone else does?

What I want to highlight is how *you* approach social media; not how social media approaches you.

Think about how susceptible you are to what you see online and how it affects your decision making. If you see a person who seems to be doing better than you, does it put you off progression, or do you keep trying? Does a six-pack or perfect bum deflate or inspire you?

Social media and the people around us have a huge influence on our lives, yet few of us can actually change that situation and some don't even notice it.

So many people are blind to the fact that the reason for their lack of ambition and drive, motivation and aspiration is because of those they keep company with – both in person and online.

Consider seriously everything you do, both online and in real life, when either socializing, working, networking, gaming, or swiping left or right:

- Start following people within your field who own the expertise and stories that inspire you.
- In the flesh, socialize with people who inhabit worlds you want to be part of.
- Put yourself in fields and environments where you can learn, grow and feel inspired by those who surround you.
- Ensure your environments positively influence you.
- Surround yourself with people who will support and boost your courage.

DON'T LET HATERS STEAL YOUR BELIEF

Accept it, there will always be people who are going to hate you. The naysayers, haters and cynics who oppose everything you do. They may be within your social circle, online, or work only a few desks away. Wherever they are, they will let you know that everything you're doing is wrong, arrogant, stupid, thoughtless, won't work, is going to fail and every other negative comment they can think of. They will try to tear the belief from within you.

Let them hate. Let them be the ones who waste their time worrying about *you* while *you* worry about your dreams. Let them expend their energy on hating. They will stagnate, while you cast off and set sail on your adventures.

Whatever you choose to do, there will always be unqualified 'experts' waffling in your ear or behind your back about how you should rethink the idea, telling you how they would do it differently, or what you should do instead. And the more successful you become, the more they will appear.

> If you can, cut these people loose and ignore their comments. Worrying too much about what others think of you will only hold you back and damage your confidence and belief.

People who hate will never know the detail of how hard you are working, the long hours you put in at night, the money you have invested, the countless hours of personal development you have committed to and everything else required to become a success. All they will see is your sudden achievements, so they spring their hate upon you.

Tell yourself, people who hate you or cast discouraging remarks are only hating themselves. They hate the fact that *they* aren't doing what you're doing. They lack the courage and belief you possess to follow through on their own inspirations and goals. Although it may seem like these people physically hate *you*, the reality is far different. They are only hating *themselves* for not acting on what inspires them.

Bar the spiteful and select few, you rarely hear of a successful actor or actress, business tycoon, politician, entrepreneur, sports star or musician throwing hate at those who follow them. Yet how often do you hear those full of jealousy and envy firing negative and damaging comments around online or behind backs?

It is unusual to find successful people slamming others who aspire to be in their position. In fact, you're more likely to witness encouragement and praise, so why would you not want to surround yourself with those people?

IT TAKES COURAGE

It takes immense courage to change your environment and surround yourself with excellence. It takes courage to ditch the negative ones you're with, for those who are more supportive and generous in knowledge and praise. It takes even greater courage to ignore the haters; hearing what they say and choosing to lock it out. But, if you can – and you will – your belief will be greatly supported.

Some of the things they said I couldn't do . . .

- Overcome my drug addiction
- Get into the marines
- Last more than a few months in training
- Be a Commando
- Go to war
- Start a business
- Speak on stage
- Write a book
- Secure a publishing deal
- Publish a book with a penguin on the cover

I remember like yesterday all the negative comments people made to me. We may brush them off but we don't forget. Sometimes it's useful to remind yourself of what the doubters have said because it can drive you forward and remind you of your success.

Remind *yourself* of this when you encounter negative people.

Take courage and own the belief that you WILL succeed.

HOW'S THE FAMILY?

Your family can be the most supportive network in the world but, equally, the most resistance and criticism can come from within the family unit. Relatives can be a wonderful source of strength but, unfortunately, they can sometimes become our biggest obstacle to evolving – and this can be extremely damaging.

If your family demonstrate little support for your quest, don't hate them for it or create conflict. Ask yourself whether they are just trying to protect you. They might still believe in you, but want to protect you from failure and keep you safe. Our families usually want to see us succeed – but in the safest and most comfortable way possible. Often, what they say sounds so negative, but they're only trying to protect and secure us.

If your family haven't bought into your dreams and ambitions it might not be because they don't think you can do it but that they aren't personally as passionate about your goals as you are. They may simply have different inspirations and priorities in life, and this isn't anyone's fault. What may be important to you might be less so to them. Never feel guilty for what you want to do, even if those closest don't seem to get it. You must do what's best for you and not anyone else. Do what you need to do to achieve your dreams, even if that means severing some contact with certain family members, whether in the short term or permanently. But remember, it's highly likely their opinions will be very different when you succeed at whatever it is you plan to achieve!

If you have a supportive family, then that's excellent. Having a family that support you can be transformative.

Take me, for example . . .

At the time of writing, I have a five-year-old at school, a wrecking ball of a two-year-old, an unbelievably supportive but always busy wife, two cars, debt, a new mortgage, a carpet-destroying cat, a hyperactive miniature labradoodle and five business ventures. My life is sometimes chaotic, my business is thriving but hectic, and the biggest thing that gets me through that is the love and support of my family. I own the most solid family foundations I could ask for and these help me to strive towards my goals.

> When you own huge inspirations and goals, when you want a larger piece of the world's pie, it's going to take great courage and belief to risk it all and take a punt at making it happen. That journey is far easier when you have your family's support and encouragement.

Some of you have children. Many of you have a partner. Most of you have overheads. Almost all of you have debt. And every single one of you will have someone or something you will have to sacrifice in order to chase your dreams.

Whether it's spending time with them, or parting ways if they don't support your dreams, it will take courage to make that decision.

Never be afraid to wave goodbye for a short while, or longer if necessary, because you will return to them improved. Anyone who matters shouldn't mind you taking short spells to work on yourself and your goals. And those who do mind, shouldn't matter.

LIVE LIFE ON THE EDGE

I wasted my years at school, messing around and not studying. I just wasn't inspired by the subjects I was being taught. But now, as clichéd as it sounds, I wish I could do it all over again. Fifteen years on, I'm obsessed with learning about what interests me – how to deliver an inspiring talk, improvement coaching and people performance.

When I conduct a talk, I enjoy putting the audience on edge with a little exercise called 'Suspicious Minds'. Up on screen I project a large picture of the legend Elvis Presley, before revealing to everyone that one seat has a yellow sticker underneath with *You* written on it. Eyes widen, fidgeting bodies try to grab a swift peek under their chairs as I deliver the news that one lucky person will be coming up on stage to sing 'Suspicious Minds', without backing music.

I do this exercise for two reasons. First, it gets everyone just as nervous as I am on stage and creates a slightly unsettled feeling among the audience, who originally thought they were safe. Second, it brings everyone out of their comfort zones immediately, raising their adrenal responses and placing them in a hypersensitive state. Suddenly, they no longer want to be in the room.

It's a good ice-breaker. Gets them sitting up, makes them concentrate and therefore helps them learn.

As we discovered earlier, we grow when we operate just outside our comfort zones. And that's exactly what I like to do with a large group of people. Placing them outside their comfort zones creates instant engagement; they become more involved in the talk, taking on board more information than maybe they would have without the exercise.

I want you to keep this trick I play on my audience in mind when you think about your comfort zone. Start setting yourself small tasks outside what you feel is comfortable in order to grow your courage. Like the people in my audiences, you need to put yourself slightly on edge, so you're ready for bigger challenges ahead and eager to embrace new things outside what you know.

As you move forward, be conscious about your comforts creeping in, pulling you back towards your old ways and habits.

When you finish this book, are you going to stick it on a shelf or continue to refer back to it, working towards your inspirations and goals?

A lot of people would do exactly that. Put their motivational book down and never return to their inspirations and goals again. This is not going to be you. You are going to keep working towards your dream, putting yourself outside your comfort zone so that you grow.

Write the following in your journal:

- 'I will not fall back into being too comfortable.'
- 'I will not allow myself to be lazy and procrastinate.'
- 'I will step outside my comfort zone to grow.'
- 'I will get there.'

NOW IT'S TIME TO ENACT

It's go time! Everything that you've learned in the Inspiration and Courage sections will be put into play in the last part of this book. You are about to enter Enactment, the crucial step towards making your dreams happen.

Feeling excited and energized, eager to go and ready for what comes? You should be. Know that I'm excited for you, too. Now is your time to take on the world and achieve. No more waiting around.

I want you to let go of whatever has been holding you back and finally believe in yourself.

> Everything you've read so far has been gearing you up to this very point – the green light for go. You've turned your inspirations into goals. You've set the goals into a plan. You've broken through the boundaries of fear. You've discovered your values. You believe in yourself and are filled with courage. You're ready to get shit done.

As you begin to progress through the third part of this book, I want you to start acting on your goals at the same time.

Use what you've written in your journal – the goal strategies you've set, your notes from the 'Pause for thought' boxes and the ICE reflection exercises – to build a bigger picture of who you are, what you want and how you're going to get it.

Don't procrastinate or wait until the end of the book to set out on your journey.

If the light fades, or you begin to wobble, remind yourself of your inspirations and why you are doing what you are doing. Have that picture printed or photo ready to pull out during a moment of darkness, because it may just save your hopes and dreams.

With little left to do, let's enact . . .

ICE reflection 7:
Simply start by putting out the bin

How many times have you gone to put something in the bin, then seen it's full and needs emptying? Instead of emptying it, you force it down with all your might, squeezing out the last little bit of space left inside.

Not all of you will do this, but I'm sure most of you do – even I find myself from time to time manipulating a crisp packet into the last pocket of space. Some of you probably leave dirty mugs on the side or ignore the dishwasher that needs emptying. We're all guilty occasionally. If you don't, then, good effort. The next part of this book should be easier for you than the rest.

However, to enhance your Commando mindset, I want you all to test yourselves and begin the 'getting the basics right' approach.

I want you to concentrate on doing the extremely mundane tasks within your life straightaway and to the highest standards.

Any time you notice the washing up on the side, do it.

When you feel like bin squashing, just take it straight out.

Reply to the emails you're about to flag as important.

Walk the dog first thing.

Do your coursework as soon as you get in.

Mow the lawn.

Get up as soon as the alarm sounds.

Make your bed when you wake up.

Do the basics right and you will feel immense pride in yourself, and build belief that you can do the bigger things.

Try it!

ENACTMENT

It has been said that adversity introduces a man to himself.
President Richard Nixon

Commandos keep going

It's 6 August 2011. I stroll into the little chill-out area of our small base and glance at the TV screen everyone is engrossed with.

British fatalities for the year so far stand at twenty-eight. And hundreds more injured. In little more than seven months. Only yesterday, twenty-two-year-old James Wright, a Royal Marine from Juliet Company, was killed by a grenade just down the road from the base we occupy.

Emotions are raw, people are tired. Every day seems like we're pissing into the wind.

The Taliban are relentless. Gunfights and IED strikes are at their height. Only the medical kit and equipment, highly trained and skilled soldiers and swift evacuations keep more people surviving horrific incidents. Motivation is not far off depletion.

As I look on – expecting to see the brave face of Marine James Wright and a report on how he heroically laid down his life – we are instead greeted with videos and images of a burning London.

'Here, Damo, look at this!' Damo steps in and joins in watching.

'What the fuck is that all about?' demands Damo, as we look on, bewildered.

'London's rioting,' says Gaz, who is watching the TV.

'Have they said anything about James from J Company yet, Gaz?' I ask.

'Nothing, mate. It's all about this at the moment,' he responds.

'Why hasn't James's news come up?' I blurt out. 'What the fuck is going on back at home? What are we doing in Afghanistan, if we can't even control our own streets?'

'Fucking joke, isn't it?' Gaz gestures. 'Makes you wonder what the point of it all is!'

Standing shocked in front of live footage of the London riots, I can't believe what I'm looking at. In several hours, we're moving out for an early evening patrol in a highly contentious area. If one of us dies, our country isn't going to have a clue.

I stroll back to our tent, delivering the news of our crumbling capital to the lads inside, while we continue to fight the War on Terror.

Everything we've been through, every person killed and injured currently seems all in vain. I begrudgingly pack my kit for the patrol – bitter, to say the least.

The mood in our tent is low, and the atmosphere is bleak – everyone senses it.

'What's up, lads?' one of our commanders asks, breaking the silence.

'We are fuming about London. No one gives a fuck about us here,' a voice blurts out.

'You not seen the news? Our country has gone tits up, while we have to carry on fighting in this fucking war,' another lad complains. 'Why should we even bother going out there later?'

The air is thick with tension. Morale is low.

'Does everyone feel this way?' one of our other commanders prompts. More marines nod in agreement.

'Well, tough. It doesn't matter what is going on at home. All that matters is that we do our jobs out on the ground and look after one another. Don't lose focus on why we are here, lads; keep your heads in the game!' His tone cuts through the tension, and his point is valid.

'Remember who you are, lads; you are Royal Marines Commandos,' another commander adds.

Our commander was absolutely right. Whatever is happening back at home has no effect on our next patrol, only we do. Our heads need to be in the game, and we must still step from the safety of our base and hunt down our enemies.

We must push distracting thoughts aside and continue to do our job to the best of our ability. We must continue to enact the values and principles that underpin the Royal Marines and our mission at hand. We must call upon and act on our Commando mindset.

ENACTMENT

↑

COURAGE

↑

INSPIRATION

8.
Get Shit Done and Keep on Going

WAITING FOR THE ACTION

When we first arrived in Afghanistan, I thought the days would be filled with aggressive fighting, followed by long nights of attacks. I assumed we would be facing a relentless barrage of assaults – wave after wave of enemy fighters attempting to penetrate the positions we defended. Although we did a dangerous job in a violent place, there was everyday life to live.

War is 90 per cent boredom, 10 per cent action – something that can make keeping going very difficult. Among the patrols, operations and battles, much of our time was spent cleaning weapons and kit, sleeping, doing sentry, eating, exercising, preparing for the next mission. Doing the relatively mundane things that took up most of our time underpinned the success of the operation; the 10 per cent action.

I think this can be applied to everyday life. A lot of big dreams and goals are made up of small, mundane tasks that can often seem irritating to do. But these little steps and tasks are pivotal – without them, the 10 per cent of action wouldn't be achievable. The marines taught me how necessary it was to get the 90 per cent correct in order to make the 10 per cent as successful as possible.

This part of the book is going to offer you advice and tools to help you enact the goals you have laid out so far. It's going to help you get through the 90 per cent to maximize your own 10 per cent. I'm not going to walk you through exact ways to enact every single one of your dreams, but I will reveal the areas in your life where you could make small changes that will empower you to achieve what you desire. I will teach you about the benefits of positive thinking and visualization, and how to deal with the inevitable adversity you will meet.

Enactment is the hardest part of the ICE process. It's easy enough to daydream about inspirations and goals, as well as how you are going to battle fear and grow your courage, but actually committing to the doing process is the hardest part for most people.

Have faith – you *will* get this done. Plough through this part as you have the rest of this book, and keep the momentum up. Constantly remind yourself of why you are doing what you are doing, and remember that simply by placing one foot in front of the other you will reach your goal.

POSITIVITY IS KEY

We all experience those glum days when we just don't feel up to it. When our minds are tired and every problem feels like a mountain to climb. When we're distracted from our goals because of a particular emotion we're feeling. Think how my Commando company was momentarily distracted by the riots in London. Sometimes negative thoughts creep in that make it hard to do the task you have set yourself that day.

How many of these days have caused you to lose focus and give up, dropping everything and leaving it for tomorrow? Days when the sofa seems like the only place of refuge can really affect your progress. The more regularly they happen, the more your self-belief and your goals will suffer.

Positivity is one of the most powerful tools in achieving success. Being positive doesn't mean you need to walk around with a great big smile on your face all the time. We're allowed our down days. But the more positive you can be about situations you face, the easier life becomes. Thinking positively will help you create new perspectives and significantly change the way you view and approach situations. For example, instead of thinking *I can't do this*, ask yourself *How can I do this?* If you want to set up a business but you think you don't have the knowledge to do so, ask yourself *how* you can gain that knowledge. Turn your destructive thought into a positive question that will help you overcome the perceived issue.

Nobody likes spending time with negative people. And nobody wants to spend time with their own negative inner voice either. In the marines, people who waste their time picking the negatives out of everything and whining about the pointless things are called 'drips' (or 'drip artists', if they do it frequently).

Do you want to be a drip? Are you friends with drips?

Remember the power of positive thinking the next time you catch yourself thinking or saying something negative. Try to switch that thought into a positive by reframing it as a question. If you find yourself surrounded by negative people, consider changing your social group – remember, you want to surround yourself with excellence.

CREATING SUCCESS WITH VISUALIZATION

In one way or another, I saw something of myself in every recruit I trained. Whether it was their previous lifestyle choices or their sheer drive and determination to become a Commando, I could empathize with them as they stepped into a completely alien world.

—Visualization exercise 1—

Visualize yourself ten years from now.

Where are you? What are you doing? What have you achieved?

Take in the sights, sounds and smells of wherever it is you are.

Feel the pride oozing from you as you reflect on the countless hours of hard work and wins along the way.

Visualize the inspirations you turned into goals to get to this point.

Does life seem good? Do you feel rewarded? Do you feel happy?

Just like me many years before, young lads with wide and worried eyes would step off the train, clutching their own ironing boards and wearing similar cheap suits as they embarked on a new adventure to earn their green beret.

I took great pride in turning civilians into Royal Marines Commandos and felt a sense of privilege that those young and eager men trusted me. In all honesty, apart from the odd few who just weren't cut out for life in the marines, I wanted all my recruits to pass Commando training. But I wouldn't make it easy. To pass training and take their place within a fighting unit, they too would need to prove they owned everything that a Royal Marine stands for: values, courageous spirit, grit, resilience – a Commando mindset.

When I first started training recruits, I had already begun reading and listening to self-development books and was enjoying unlocking my own potential. I also had two good friends on my training team, Charlie and Richy, who adored Tony Robbins, Brian Tracy, John C. Maxwell and all the other big motivational hitters, just like I did.

We realized that the new knowledge we were discovering for ourselves could also greatly benefit our Commando recruits. So we began implementing snapshots and hacks from these motivational giants, incorporating them into training. Goal-setting and habit creation suddenly became part of our troop's syllabus.

GET SHIT DONE AND KEEP ON GOING

Out of all the tips and techniques we imparted to our recruits from the books we read, visualization seemed to crop up again and again – a powerful aid in imagining yourself getting to where you wanted to go.

I vividly remember imagining what it would be like to place that green beret on my head for the first time, the touch of its cloth energizing me, standing proud in my immaculate uniform. So we would ask our recruits to do the same and imagine what it would feel like to finish training, earning their place as a Royal Marines Commando. We would pick these moments wisely, often when they were depleted with exhaustion, wet and very cold – it worked best when adversity was present.

—Visualization exercise 2 —

Conduct the first visualization exercise once more. This time, however, go into greater detail, following the three steps below and putting yourself in the position of success with more clarity.

As you do, imagine each emotion and feeling; absorb every ounce of the success you envisage and really try to imagine yourself there.

Step one – Locate a quiet space you find peaceful. There's little point pitching up in a busy café or trying this on the bus. You need to feel relaxed and at ease, with no distractions.

Step two – Clear your mind and tune in to your imagination. Take a few deep breaths and relax, while focusing on your breathing. After clearing your mind, enter step three.

Step three – Imagine your goals in greater detail. Visualize the sights of your new environment and position, the sounds of everything around you and the people you are with. Create collages in your head of everything you see and hold on to how positive you feel.

When you're done, write down the emotions, feelings and happiness you felt throughout. Place what you've written next to your goals.

Conduct the visualization exercise as frequently as you find helpful.

Visualization is an incredibly powerful tool to help you stay focused as it allows you to interact with the future and tap into the joy of achieving what you've set out to do. It is a crucial technique to employ when times of challenge arise and you lose sight of the finish line.

YOU ARE A PROBLEM SOLVER

Every professional runner imagines crossing the finish line first. Every entrepreneur visualizes successfully achieving funding, growth and, hopefully, wealth. Every actor imagines themselves accepting an Oscar or a Bafta.

But visualization isn't just about thinking about the final goal. You also need to consider the journey towards it, imagining the exact pathway that will get you there.

When thinking about success, try seeing yourself more as a problem solver rather than a daydreamer. Visualize the strategy you have and what you will need to do to complete the goal.

I've used marathon running as an example on several occasions already. I'm going to use it again. In the diagrams on pages 181 and 182, see the difference in your thought processes when you compare Fantasy visualization (picturing *just* the end result) and Simulation (picturing *how* you'll get there).

FANTASY VISUALIZATION

MENTAL PICTURE ⟶	REAL-LIFE EVENT ⟶	OUTCOME
'I'm a fit person who can complete a race.'	'It's raining. Shall I train today?'	'Maybe I'll put it off. I'm not a bad person for doing so.'
'I have already accomplished something similar before.'	'I'm already fit, I know I can finish the race in respectable time.'	'I'll train tomorrow.'
'I enjoy the positive feelings of self-image.'		'I'm already fit, another day won't hurt.'

Fantasy visualization is *just* picturing the result of the goal, without considering the journey towards it. That may look like standing on the podium, counting the money, getting the job or whatever. Fantasy visualization is allowing your imagination to run wild and think of the glory, not the task. It is good to visualize yourself as successful, but it's important to spend more time visualizing the process.

A sports star clearly imagines lifting the trophy, but they also run through the exact process of what they will do in the game to get there. The penalty kick, sprinting technique, the tactics of that specific match, their coach's strategy. Specific scenarios they can visualize that build towards the end goal – this is Simulation.

SIMULATION

As you can see, Simulation focuses much more on the process than the result. It is exactly what the sports star does, focusing on the strategy and practical application of skill and motivation, rather than the reward alone.

Just as I felt in the first days of training – when my corporal said I wouldn't make it past week two – I too needed to think less about the green beret and more about the strategy of the journey there – getting through only the next week. Hence why I broke the whole course into small, manageable goals and focused on one week at a time.

MENTAL PICTURE ➡	REAL-LIFE EVENT ➡	OUTCOME
'I'm going to train everyday, come rain or shine.'	'It's raining. Shall I train today?'	'I have planned for days like this, I will go for a run.'
'I am willing to reverse the challenges I'll face.'	'I'm already fit, I know I can finish the race in respectable time.'	'I said to myself that no matter what, I will train daily.'
'I will prepare myself for moments I'll need to push myself.'		

— Pause for thought —

As well as imaging the end goal, where else could you focus the attention of your visualization techniques?

What part of your plan and strategy can you visualize?

Write down a few bullet points for one or two of your goals and consider areas where visualizing would benefit your motivation.

NEVER SETTLE FOR THE BARE MINIMUM

The Commando mindset comprises lots of different elements – the ICE model, positive thinking, setting realistic goals, pushing past your comfort zone. Another important principle in the Commando mindset that will help you on your journey to enactment is to go beyond the minimum that is expected, and this may come from a simple nudge by someone next to you who is equally determined. *Surround yourself with excellence* – is that phrase ringing bells again?

In the small teams of six to eight people Commandos often worked alongside, bonds were tight and strong. This encouraged us to work hard for one another, and not just when we were together. Knowing you are part of such a highly trained team forced us to work out that bit harder in our spare time and read up on tactics, so we were even better equipped when we formed a unit. *What you do in the shadows matters most.*

I remember one of my senior commanders once saying: 'Always try to exceed yourself on a daily basis, even if it is only by a little bit,' a phrase that couldn't be more apt to achieving the Commando mindset.

Constantly try to better yourself every day. If you encounter a situation where you can be part of (or form) a group with a similar mindset – for example undertaking a project at work, training in the gym or as a member of a sports team – perhaps you too can create a unit in which everyone works for each other, not only when you're together but also when you are separated.

> We all own an ability to push ourselves beyond our perceived limitations, whether it's a mental or a physical challenge.

Stay clear of the trap many people fall into, the trap of doing the bare minimum required to see through a task. Average people do this, committing themselves to *only* what is required, instead of going that *extra* bit further – resting on their laurels.

'But what do you mean, Ben? I thought you said that, once we've done everything needed for the day, we have earned our time on the sofa.'

In a way, this is correct and I'm not stopping you. Feel free to relax once you've done everything you need to for the day. That's your reward.

However, keep this in mind – what you set yourself to do is the bare minimum, no matter how much you task yourself. Also – and this is important – those who adopt the Commando mindset always seek to do that little bit more. It feels far more rewarding when you lie on your sofa knowing you did everything you needed to *and a bit extra*.

If you can get into the habit of not settling for the bare minimum, keeping going for that extra yard, you will propel yourself towards success.

You will discover more and more small wins that will boost your positivity and fill you with pride. You'll be rewarded with more frequent and higher doses of your four pleasure chemicals. Don't turn your journey of success into a box-ticking exercise; turn it into a way to exceed expectations.

Run a few hundred metres further, do a few extra reps, write another paragraph, call half a dozen more potential clients.

Chip away at your goals while your competitors rest around you. Be willing to go that little bit further than everyone else.

ICE reflection 8:
What more can you do?

Take your journal and write the heading, 'That little bit more'.

For each of your goals, I want you to write one task you'll have to do daily that will count towards it.

It could simply be twenty minutes' exercise or calling fifteen prospective clients. They're your goals. Only you will know what to do each day to make them happen.

Now, for each daily goal, write a short promise next to it.

For example: *I need to run for twenty minutes today, but I promise to run for twenty-five.* Or *I need to call fifteen prospective clients today, but I'll ring twenty.*

Royal Marines Commando training is eight months long and classed as the world's toughest infantry course. Naturally, there's a bare minimum that needs to be done in order to become a Commando. But every marine will always do that bit more to ensure they're at their peak, not just scraping by.

Never settle for second best. Always push a little further.

SEVEN ACTION TIPS FOR ENACTMENT

Often, it is the simplest tweaks within our daily routines that have the biggest impact on our ability to get things done. Below are seven ideas to increase your effectiveness which have all helped me to enact my goals. I am confident you'll find some value in these tips and that some if not all of them will help you enact yours.

Action tip 1: Take time off tech

- Give yourself a digital holiday.
- Switch off tech for a day, or even a weekend.
- Enjoy being human again.

During my time as a Commando instructor, my team and I would ensure our recruits would not use their phones or laptops after they had returned from a long and arduous exercise in the field until all weapons, kit and themselves were clean; something which could take up to a whole night.

Keeping them away from their phones and tech forced them to talk to each other. It forced them to reflect. It forced them to bond. It would allow them time to digest and discuss both negative and positive elements of the exercise, iron out any creases or laugh about something together.

Equally, they paid full attention to what they were doing, and could get their weapons and kit cleaned without becoming distracted by what was online. They were being effective, even after their exercise was finished.

Tech is an everyday part of our lives now, it's a necessity. Emails and phones, internet and social media can all help towards our quests. But are you using them at the right time? Balance your usage to ensure you are being at your most effective, and try not to let it become a distraction. Check out the book *Digital Minimalism*, by Cal Newport, if you want to learn more about how to do a digital detox and transform your technology use.

Aeroplane Mode: That small little aeroplane symbol on your phone is a great aid to enactment. At the gym? Aeroplane mode. Reading? Aeroplane mode. Spending time with your children? Aeroplane mode. Finalizing an important document? Aeroplane mode.

Allow that tiny little plane to transport so many of your distractions away.

Action tip 2: Wake up earlier

- Give yourself that extra hour.
- Beat your competition to the rise.

One of the most common reasons given for not being able to get things done is a lack of time. So, give yourself a bit more.

I'm not suggesting you tire yourself out. As we've discovered, good sleep is crucial for your health and wellbeing and keeps you productive. But ask yourself, if you are struggling to fit everything into one day, are you making the best use of your time?

Do you lie in bed for an hour after you wake up, checking your phone or watching TV? Just by getting up an hour earlier you immediately allow yourself some room in your day to check your emails, go for that run, read an extra chapter, or simply spend some more time with those you love.

Do you decide to go to bed in the evening and then waste the next hour watching late-night TV or randomly surfing the net?

Kicking those habits will enable you to create some extra time in the day when you can again concentrate on what's important: your goals and aspirations.

Action tip 3: Exercise

- Up your heart rate, sweat it out.
- Clear your thoughts, energize your body.

Exercise is the backbone of being a Commando. One of my former sergeants used to say, 'Troop, a day without exercise is like a day without sunshine.'

Exercise invigorates the mind and body, releasing those awesome pleasure chemicals, making us feel great. Even better, if you can exercise in the morning, you truly set yourself up for the day.

Simply increasing your heart rate in the morning is linked to a better mood and higher levels of productivity – exactly what we need to enact. It also leaves you feeling sharp and awakened, allowing you to own your mind and make clearer decisions throughout the day. This will help you keep on track with your goals.

Action tip 4: Go booze-free

- Kick the drink for a month.
- Save on calories, money and the time you waste when hungover.
- Feel your motivation return.

Do it, I dare you. Go a month without alcohol and see how you feel by the end.

The benefits of abstinence are so drastic that many people find themselves staying off the drink longer than they intended.

You'll be getting benefits to your sleep cycle, decision making and problem solving in the first week. Fewer headaches by week two, and better circulation. Week three sees the health benefits going deeper, lower blood pressure, keener eyesight. By week four, your skin is healthier, your liver's had a great holiday – and, hopefully, so has your wallet, as you'll have saved on average £100. What would you rather do with that money?

Aside from the obvious effects, cutting down on the booze enables you to wake up with a clearer head and more energy, helping you focus on what matters. This alone will help you with Action tips 2 and 3.

You're on a mission to achieve something (your goal), so give yourself a head start by reducing hangovers and fuzzy heads. Awakening fresh and revitalized will immediately allow you to start the day on the right foot.

(If you're not a big drinker, perhaps you're a smoker, in which case you could consider giving up the nicotine. This tip aligns to that equally well: clearer head, more money, healthier body.)

Action tip 5: Focus on one thing at a time

- Avoid too much multitasking.
- Concentrate on one thing, then move on to the next.
- Keep that clarity.

When that overwhelming feeling occurs that you're doing too much, just take a step back and concentrate on one thing at a time.

Admittedly, life is phenomenally fast paced, and sometimes you may find you *need* to spin a few plates at the same time. It might be that you have several projects on the go at once, and it may be impossible to manage them one at a time.

However, really try to understand what could be more effectively balanced in your life, and make an effort to focus on doing things in manageable chunks.

I often found young recruits who struggled to keep their kit up to the standards expected because they were trying to do too much at once. Recruits who tried to clean all their kit at the same time, bouncing around from item to item, lacked concentration and always failed. They overloaded themselves, resulting in a poor standard.

The most diligent recruits and marines did things systematically. They would set themselves a time to clean their weapon and work tirelessly to make it as clean as possible within the allotted time. They would allocate a set time for cleaning each item of kit, ensuring they never dropped their standard. They wouldn't flick-flack between items, doing a bit on one, then a bit on the next, and so on.

Ensuring you complete the task at hand before moving on to the next will naturally enable you to be far more efficient in getting things done.

Action tip 6: Just say no!

- Give some time to Number One.
- You can't please everyone, so don't try to.
- Balance is key.

It's one of the toughest things to say to someone, but sometimes you just have to say no.

I am not encouraging you to walk into work and refuse when your boss asks you to complete a new project by the end of the week. What I am encouraging you to think about is what are you saying yes to? Are you taking on too much just to be polite, or to help someone out?

People can take advantage of your generosity with time, or at times do not realize they are creating a burden on someone else by asking them to help with their task.

Make sure you are giving yourself enough time to do what *you* need to do; not what others need you to do.

Our careers and lives will often require us to help other people and say yes, but from now on, ensure you are agreeing to undertake only the correct things, and that you are leaving time for you. If saying yes will be bad for you, just say 'NO!'

Action tip 7: Plan for uninterrupted time

- Put some time aside and block it off.
- Appreciate some 'you' time.

Whether you plan for thirty minutes' 'you' time a day, three hours a week, or one day a month, block it out in the diary and make it all about you.

This block in the calendar is for you, to go and do that training run or hit the gym. It is an opportunity to continue your business plan or make those phone calls to important clients. If you live a very busy life, this is the moment you can make a bit of headway towards one or two of your goals.

I would suggest that you look at putting aside a solid two-hour chunk a week and use it however you see fit. Make sure it is about you, though, not about your day job or even your family; it is *your* selfish moment, so enjoy it. It will help you get done what *you* want to do.

Helicopter Assault Force #2, 15 May 2011

Our Chinook charges through the night sky. It's 4 a.m., but still dark, a sprinkling of stars being the only source of light.

The aircraft shudders violently and I feel my ears pop as we descend. It's early in our tour, and we're hurtling towards our most dangerous mission yet – to occupy a known enemy village, rumoured to be an IED-making facility.

'Two minutes!' the door gunner yells. We take turns in passing the message on.

Sounds of the rotor blades slowing down, the helicopter readying to land.

'One minute!' the gunner bellows again. Everyone lifts one finger and shows it to the next person.

We're packed in like sardines, our weapons and kit filling all the spare space between our bodies. Laden down in my seat, I try to edge my way forward, ready to stand for touchdown. I don't want to be caught struggling if a hail of enemy fire enters the helicopter. I need to be ready.

Again, the aircraft shudders. The nose points rapidly towards the sky as the experienced pilot touches the rear of the bird down before landing the nose.

Every person clambers up, helping the next. And we hurry off the back of the Chinook to take up our positions in the field.

Sudden quiet. The aircraft is gone. Only the faint noise of radio chatter can be heard. But something is wrong. Our troop has landed in the correct position, but the second troop of thirty marines who will be conducting the operation with us has been dropped off in the adjacent field. The wrong one. An area known to be surrounded by IEDs.

Without the other troop, we can't complete the mission. It's a collective operation where every person counts. And so the difficult but necessary decision is made for them to navigate over to us. We will enter the village together. Yet between us and them is a dense treeline, likely laced with hidden bombs.

It's tense. The air thick with anticipation. Still bodies. Dawn is nearing. Kneeling, we watch through our NVGs (night-vision goggles) as fellow marines begin the daunting walk. Nothing but silence.

I switch knees, trying to get comfortable under my heavy kit and ease the already present aches.

Stretching my neck, I stare upwards, briefly relieving the pressure in my spine. Seen through my NVGs, the sky contains twice the number of stars visible to the naked eye. For a second, I'm perplexed by its enormity and my own irrelevance.

Bang! A loud explosion snaps me into reality. I brace for an immediate hail of bullets. *What the fuck was that?* I think, frantically scouring the compounds through my NVGs.

It must be the enemy. There's no way they didn't hear us land – we're little more than a hundred metres from their door.

Is this an ambush? Yet no one moves, assessing where the noise has come from, controlling all emotions, thinking with clarity.

Distant screams sound. Voices start yelling commands throughout the other troop, their tone filled with controlled panic. I look over through the grainy green image I see through my goggles, only just able to identify a few of them.

'Contact IED, lads. No one move!' Vicey orders next to me.

My stomach clamps with fear as I realize what's happened – someone has trodden on an IED.

'Someone's been hit!' Vicey continues calmly. 'Sit tight, lads,' he commands. 'This place is fucking littered with IEDs.'

My focus moves to the ground, wondering how close the

nearest one is. Suddenly, a feeling of claustrophobia engulfs me as I imagine the field around us now filled with life-altering bombs.

As I turn my attention to the other troop once more, I feel so helpless. Our friends are stranded in the wrong field, now dealing with our injured colleagues – our pals. *Fuck, I hope it isn't that bad. Just cuts and bruises – maybe a lucky escape? Please say it was just a small device and that they're all OK.* But my thinking is wishful.

'Stand by for names, lads,' Vicey warns. He's receiving news of each casualty.

'Ranners!'

'Spoony . . .' he pauses.

'. . . And Deano.'

My heart sinks. *Fucking three!* Less than an hour ago, we were safe and none the wiser. Messing around, replacing boredom with mockery and jibes.

'What are their injuries?' I hesitantly ask Vicey, not wanting to hear his reply.

'Don't know yet,' he responds bluntly, keen to shut me up, pressing his earpiece further in, listening intently to what's happening.

'Prepare to move, lads, we're going in.' Vicey's tone swiftly changes from dampened spirit to angry warrior. We ready ourselves to execute the plan.

'AEs are breaching now,' he continues, referring to the forward party of assault engineers. 'Stand by, stand by.'

Another explosion booms. This time, it's controlled by our guys. The AEs have blown a hole in the first compound. The explosion's echo repeats over and over, then it fades. If the Taliban have managed to sleep through our arrival, they are certainly up now.

I grab my weapon and move with the troop. We enter the compounds, Taliban now metres away. My mind is fixed on the mission.

Our friends are hurt, but there's little room for emotions right now. Their only place is at the back of our minds.

We have a job to do.

Twenty hours later, we gather in the small outdoor dining area back at Patrol Base Folad – a relatively safe haven from where we conduct our operations.

The day has been grim, violent and bloody. It's the first time some of us have witnessed death on the battlefield caused by our own hands. The characters of many have changed for ever within a single few hours.

Exhausted bodies, covered in sweat, mud and blood, drop their heavy kit and slump in the rickety chairs. Standing before us is our unit's CO. With him, the regimental sergeant major and our chaplain – rare faces to see in our base at midnight. I know what's coming.

'Guys, I just want to say, fucking good effort out there!' the CO says with genuine pride, yet tinged with an air of anger and aggression. 'So far, what we know, you killed sixteen insurgents and have made a considerable impact on enemy fighters in that area.'

His words have weight, but seemingly fall on deaf ears. Instead, lads are staring into the abyss through cold and empty eyes.

Our CO senses the atmosphere – everyone needs putting out of their misery.

'Boys,' his tone lowers to express both empathy and emotion. 'As you know, Marines Scott Ransley and James Spooner were injured in the explosion this morning. Both are OK, although doctors aren't sure about Scott's eyesight. But they will make a recovery.' He pauses and takes a breath.

'However, I'm sorry to say, Marine Nigel Dean Mead lost his life this morning in the blast. Those who treated Deano did an incredible job, and I . . .'

The CO's voice begins drifting away. I can hear nothing but my own thoughts. I watch drained faces drop – some silent, others crying, as everyone absorbs the terrible news.

We have suffered our heaviest loss. We have lost the first of what will be many friends.

Adversity is upon us. For the first time in the tour, we are reminded of the stark realities of warfare. To succeed with the effect we desperately desire, this type of adversity will become the norm and is something we must all face.

But now is the time for mourning. Sleep easy, Nigel Dean 'Deano' Mead – Commando. Hero. Friend. Brother.

ENACTMENT

↑

COURAGE

↑

INSPIRATION

9.
Bouncing Back from Adversity

ADVERSITY IS EVERYWHERE

Deano's death hit us all like a train. It cut every single one of us to the core. The talented nineteen-year-old sniper was a loveable rogue who spent hours listening to the DJ Deadmau5, wore different coloured laces in his trainers and drank sambuca like it was going out of fashion. He was the life and soul of the party, yet at the same time a truly professional, diligent and tenacious Royal Marines Commando. He lost his life doing the job he loved and would have rather sacrificed his own than see harm come to any one of his fellow marines.

Losing Deano on that fateful day was what woke me up to the harsh reality of what we were doing. Up until that point, my knowledge of war and the horrific adversity it casts upon those involved was limited to what I had read in papers and watched on the news. But seeing his bloodstained kit and the emotionless stares of my friends who had treated him forced me to grow up within a split second. It made me realize the importance of learning through adversity and being made stronger by that which attempts to set us back.

'Some of you will be injured. And some of you will be killed. When it happens, just make sure that the rest of you are there, ready to support one another. You will all need it.'

These were the parting words of my troop commander in training, before we left for our units. They may seem morbid to you, but to us it was the world we lived in, and he was right. There is no secret formula that is taught to us for how to behave when someone is hurt. All we can do is be there for one another and maintain the tightest support network possible.

On the bad days on operations, we would light a small fire, sit around and share funny stories of those who had been killed or injured. It was really important that we all knew how the others were feeling, let it all out and deal with challenge and shock collectively and immediately. It was important not to let isolation become the killer of our minds, and to work through the adversity together.

You will likely have experienced something that has caused you to question whether you should carry on or not. It may have been a physical or psychological challenge, or possibly both; but you will, in one way or another, no matter how small or big, have experienced an adverse situation in your life. Perhaps on more than one occasion. Even this week, in your work or your family situation, you may have encountered adversity on a multitude of different levels.

Across our planet, adversity is everywhere: catastrophic disasters, financial crashes, extreme weather, war, terror, fatalities, homelessness, redundancies; anywhere you look, someone or something is suffering. Some people face adversity regularly, others less often; but, without question, we *all* face it at some point in our lives.

—Pause for thought—

- How do *you* deal with adversity?
- How do you approach the negative situations you face?
- Do you challenge them head on?
- Do you accept? Or do you blame?

Write down your thoughts in a few sentences.

CHEERFULNESS IN THE FACE OF ADVERSITY

You may remember back in the 'My Story' section I introduced the four spirits the Royal Marines endeavour to embody:

- *Courage*
- *Determination*
- *Unselfishness*
- *Cheerfulness*

All four are invaluable, but here I want to highlight the last one – *cheerfulness.*

As commandos, we expand this to *cheerfulness in the face of adversity.* We make humour the heart of morale – getting through our hardest times by laughing, or trying to see the lighter side.

I can't count the amount of times I've looked to my left or right during some of my most challenging moments, to see a muddy and equally fatigued face staring back at me sporting a huge grin. Smiles that trigger my own, when I realize I'm not the only one in the situation.

Positive people have such a profound effect on themselves and others, often enabling those around them to muster up that extra bit of courage they may need to crack on.

I have laughed for hours on end with some of my closest friends on some of the hardest days, proving that you can always find cheerfulness in the darkest of times. Even if you're alone, although it's trickier, you can laugh at a dire situation rather than lament. Try it and see if it helps.

Ever gone into work after a blazing row with your partner, to find that a close friend can immediately cheer you up and your argument rapidly fades to something distant and stupid? Maybe it only takes a brief giggle over a cup of tea, but that humour and laughter have a far longer and more positive impact than their duration. They can cheer you up for the whole day. *What did the zero say to the eight? Nice belt!* See, it's easy to laugh. (Please say you laughed . . .)

If you cast your mind back to the pleasure chemicals, endorphins are released not just during times of pain but also when you're having a good chuckle. When you're stressed or sad, those endorphins will suppress your negative feelings and allow you to feel good again. Positive thinking is one of the most powerful tools in helping you pick yourself up from hard times and get moving again.

— Pause for thought —

Write down in your journal a time that made you laugh so hard your belly hurt, or a memory that brings you immense happiness.

In your head, revisit that moment again and just let yourself go. Allow your mind to wander as you enjoy the moment you identify as one of your happiest.

When you have finally stopped laughing or smiling, I want you to notice how you feel. Think about what's happened to any negativity or stress you may have had before you started. Has it disappeared? Or, at least been suppressed for now?

Hopefully, this worked for you. For a brief moment, you were able to distract your mind with undivided happiness. It's a simple-to-use trick that can have a profound impact on your thinking.

Imagine learning to do that more regularly. Remember back to the first chapter when we thought about the final wishes of people who are dying: *I wish I'd let myself be happier.*

How to overcome

Afghanistan and life within the marines taught many lessons, but the most vital one I took away was that nothing gets solved with excuses and you have to take responsibility for yourself if you're to overcome a huge challenge.

That mission on 15 May 2011 brought to the surface many distressing feelings that could have possibly hindered our abilities to soldier. Though we hadn't been told Deano was dead, we all knew the young and active teenager had suffered extremely traumatic injuries that would forever change his life.

As young men, many of us executed controlled yet extreme violence for the first time that day, killing in action sixteen members of the Taliban. We ran out of almost all our resources and ammunition. Yet the grim realization of what IEDs do to the human body brought us all back to reality immediately. We were surrounded by the enemy, surrounded by IEDs. Adversity blighted the operation, but that didn't mean we let it take control. It was the risk we faced. It was also the risk we signed up for – nothing and nobody was to blame.

Your very own missions – those of your goals – will carry great risks; huge risks!

Things will go wrong that cannot be helped and you will be forced to decide how to respond.

Will you hide in a ditch and hope it all passes?

Or do you get up and fight on?

Do you control those adrenal responses, or do you allow them to control you?

Success stems from the ability to adapt and overcome. You must be prepared to do this.

—Exercise – overcoming adversity—

Pick a moment in your life that stands out above the rest, which tested your grit and determination and took you some time to overcome.

What single moment do you cast your mind back to, which pushed you harder than the rest?

What made it adverse? What were your emotions during and after it? Did you feel angry, sad or bitter?

How did you overcome it? Did you adapt quickly to the situation? Or did it take you a long time to overcome it? Did you stall and try not to face it? Did you overcome it at all?

Whatever your method for dealing with the emotional burdens that specific moment you just chose brought, did you notice that nothing was solved until you acted? Blaming someone else or offering excuses only erect barriers to dealing with the issue. Nothing is ever solved until you decide to act.

If you want to stand above the average, you must own the mental fortitude that enables you to look beyond what you face, evading the negativity that keeps so many bound to adversity.

It may seem as if I'm being blunt about the situations you have faced or will face. As though there's little emotion or care for the adversity you've been through. This is not the case. However, the Commando mindset includes zero sympathy for the barriers people erect that prevent them from solving their problems.

LEARNING AND GROWING THROUGH CHALLENGE

Looking back at how you face challenge means you can understand why you felt as you did, how you dealt with it and, most importantly, reflect on how you overcame it.

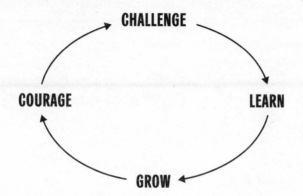

Think back to part two of the ICE model, Courage, and how developing courage grows your self-belief and vice versa. The same cyclical relationship is true for overcoming challenges – when you are challenged, you learn and grow and therefore build up courage and become better equipped to take on the next challenge. You'll pass through a cycle of growth again and again – always learning from your setbacks and growing each time you face adversity.

ARA – ACCEPT, REMOVE, ADAPT

When my patrol was blown up later in the tour, I struggled for a long time to comprehend what had happened to us. I felt guilt, pity and shame. I was blaming myself.

Years on from that incident, my friend Gav – who sustained horrific injuries during the explosion – said to me in his dry Manchester accent, 'We did our utmost on that tour, and we should be proud. Shit happens, but it's what we do next that makes us who we are.'

A light bulb switched on in my head. I suddenly owned a profound understanding of what we should do during and after adversity strikes.

Gav's observation led me to speak to people in the military, successful athletes and leaders in the business world, and ask them about how they respond to the unique challenges they face.

Though from different disciplines, most of the people I spoke to seemed to adopt a natural process that was made up of three parts. The process was about *accepting* what has happened, *removing* unwanted emotions and *adapting* to the situation at hand.

ACCEPT
Immediately accept what has happened

REMOVE
Try and remove unwanted emotion

ADAPT
Have clarity and make a decision

Accept

This is a very tricky first hurdle, but you must accept that what's happened actually has happened. There's no going back, the past cannot be changed. So the sooner you accept, the clearer you'll be able to think. The more immediate your processing of the situation, the easier you'll find it to discover a solution.

Granted, every adverse situation will differ from the next and each person's response will vary. Accepting the death of a relative is completely different from accepting a missed deadline; but, whatever the situation, you must accept it has happened.

Think back to what sprung to mind when I asked you about your toughest ever challenge, or most adverse situation. When did your acceptance kick in? Was it instantaneous? Or did you prolong the time it took to accept what had happened?

When you face adversity and challenge, it's important to gather facts immediately. Use the Condor moment (page 77) to help you process the event:

- Pause
- Think
- Process

- Remind
- Decide

Often when a shocking event took place, I would immediately look to my commanders, trying to emulate their behaviours and reactions. They were always so calm and collected, taking in their stride whatever was thrown our way. This kind of graceful acceptance was infectious and necessary because it kept us alive when something really shit happened.

Remove

Now, before anyone jumps down my throat for being heartless, assuming I am encouraging you to be emotionless, I'm not! Emotion plays a large role in our decision making and can often help us make vital choices during moments of stress and panic. At times, the limbic system within our brains must use emotions in order to make swift decisions to help us survive – it can be an extremely important response.

By suggesting that you try to remove emotion during adverse situations, I'm encouraging you to put to one side the emotions that can cloud your thought process. To accept what has happened, we must momentarily remove emotion from the situation. In our world, when something terrible happened there was often little you could do but accept it. We had to face facts and crack on with the mission, returning to any pain or grieving later. Sometimes you have to keep ploughing through and remove all emotion from the occasion, even if it feels very uncomfortable at the time.

When you're faced with a setback or challenge and you want to stop because it's difficult or it hurts, remember you are doing this for a reason, you're passionate about what you're trying to achieve, and you own the courage and tenacity to see this through.

Adapt

Finally, you must adapt to the situation. Earlier in the book I referenced Carol Dweck's two types of mindset – the growth mindset and the fixed mindset – and how those with the fixed mindset deem challenge as something to be avoided, giving up early on obstacles, viewing effort as fruitless, criticism as an attack and the success of others as a threat; all they want is to *look* smart and *look* like they never fail.

> Growth mindset is seen as intelligence that can be developed by those who embrace challenge, persist in the face of setbacks, use effort as the path to mastery, learn from criticism and find inspiration and lessons in the success of others. This is the ability to adapt.

When using the Condor moment during adversity, you give yourself time to assess your next decision. Whether a physical or psychological situation, you can always adapt to it.

How can you get over or go through, around or under the wall?

With the Commando mindset, you'll always find a way.

Once you've accepted the situation and removed unwanted emotions, adapting to the challenge becomes easier.

Although it may be difficult at the time, try to see what can be learned from the experience.

Once you learn to harness this rule effectively, adversity and every setback you encounter will become more of a lesson than a hindrance.

Accept → *Remove* → *Adapt*

BUILDING RESILIENCE

The ARA method will also help you to build resilience.

> **Resilience (noun)** The capacity to recover quickly from difficulties; toughness.

Adversity, trauma, threats, stress and major changes will all encourage you to be more resilient when dealing with them.

Resilience is about the ability to cope with the adverse situations you will inevitably face.

Resilience depends on your rational thinking ability and your physical and mental health.

Resilience is your coping method for bouncing back when setbacks strike.

You may find yourself more resilient in some areas of your life than others. I am resilient to spending months away from my family in unfamiliar, uncomfortable and hostile environments. Though I may not like it, I can still cope with it. You might not.

On the other hand, you may be more resilient than me to uncertain fluctuations in business, able to cope effectively with the instability of your field better than I could.

We all have different ways of dealing with different situations, but the true measure of resilience is how easily you are able to return to your original state, how you minimize the damage of a setback and how great an impact an adverse event has on your life. That's my definition.

Stretch an elastic band too far and it snaps. Stretch an elastic band to its limit and it returns to its original position, ready to be stretched again and again. It will remain resilient. The more easily it snaps, the less resilient it is.

SIX COMMANDO RESILIENCE RULES

The Commando mindset is steeped in resilience. Throughout my Royal Marines career, I've been privileged to witness hundreds, if not thousands of elite soldiers display immense resilience.

Sometimes I saw it in a physical beasting during training, or when the sergeant major removed a weekend's leave for a 'fast ball' (a short-notice task). Often, I saw soldiers display it when fighting in fierce and bloody warzones, witnessing their close friends' injuries and deaths.

And I've been able to observe and assess what helps these characters develop their mindsets and grow their resilience through difficult times.

Take a look at the six Commando resilience rules below. Every one of these rules contributes towards improving resilience – and, ultimately, to owning the Commando mindset. Some of them will be familiar as I've touched upon them already, but some are completely new. All of them will maximize your potential for success.

Rule 1: Find and use your values

Your values are the backbone to resilience

- Forgotten them already? Don't see the importance of values?
- Go back to Inspiration and read chapter 3 again.
- A Commando mindset is built from good, strong personal values that uphold everything you stand for.
- Your values keep you aligned and remind you what you stand for when trouble strikes.
- In dark and uncertain times, you need this moral compass to guide you when your character is tested.
- Your values help you say no when you should and follow through on what you believe in.
- Your values make you stronger in putting aside unwanted feelings and emotions, staying with what you truly live by.

Rule 2: Look after yourself

Strong physical and mental health feeds resilience

- Keeping physically and mentally fit?
- Doing enough daily exercise to get those awesome pleasure chemicals boosting you for the day?
- If so, you're building up the strength in your immune system, which can often take a hefty knock during adversity.
- A strong and resilient immune system equips your body and mind to handle stress during adversity.

- Physical activity also allows you to push and demonstrate both your physical and mental capabilities.
- Exercise isn't easy but, if you aren't testing how far you can push your mind and body, you're not growing your resilience.
- Pushing yourself, both physically and mentally, helps you find new coping methods, growing confidence and courage.

Rule 3: Own a purpose

Whatever drives you improves your resilience

- What is it that's really driving you?
- Think you've got the correct inspirations and goals?
- Are you doing them for the right reasons? Are they truly you?
- Are they meaningful and aligned to what and who you are?
- Purpose gives you that extra bit more mental strength when difficulty strikes.
- A greater sense of purpose makes you far more capable of dealing with stress, pressure, challenge and adversity.
- Link your inspirations to your purpose to help maintain focus.
- Owning a purpose is fundamental for achieving what you set out to do – it is *why* you are so committed.

Rule 4: Surround yourself with the right people

Like-minded people support your resilience

- Are you surrounding yourself with excellence?
- Are you part of a strong and positive network?
- Who are the people you can go to who can be trusted and will support you?
- When you're part of a tight community where people trust and support one another, you're in the right community.
- You're there for them, they're there for you. It's mutual.
- Knowing someone has your back makes you far more driven to take action and risk failure.

- You're confident the support is there for you when required.
- Surrounding yourself with the right people who are always there for you builds resilience.

Rule 5: Accept change

Keeping comfort at bay stokes your resilience

- Stagnating in the same life routines?
- Think change is avoidable?
- Change is inevitable! And staying in your comfort zone restricts your ability to push into fear, to learn and to grow.
- If you want to succeed at what you do, make change an integral part of your life.
- Success comes when you're willing to change and adapt.
- Allow yourself to think clearly, always trying to identify and underpin the positives in the change.
- Change builds your resilience by exposing you to the new and the difficult.
- Remind yourself of a time when you excelled because you changed what you were doing.
- Consider again the ARA method – accept, remove, adapt.

Rule 6: Keep striving

Focusing on the next goal fosters resilience

- Got where you want to be?
- Completed your current set of goals?
- Look for new paths in life, discover the next big inspiration.
- Always have a new target or an objective to work towards.
- Keep striving for more, ready to focus on the next goal.
- Staying focused and motivated is part of a long journey through continuing challenge and adversity.
- Your mental fortitude and ability to keep going will build your resilience.

- Striving will keep you determined. Being determined builds courage. And courage enables you to achieve more.
- Build your resilience through facing challenge along the way and ultimately discovering success.

NEVER GIVE UP!

This chapter may seem the toughest one to get through with little inspiration sprinkled along the way to keep you motivated – yet I make no apologies. Adversity is something you must deal with. It's a vital topic that must be covered. You're going to face masses of adversity. The more extravagant and larger your goals, the more adversity you are going to face.

Embrace the challenges that will come your way and never be put off.

Take confidence in the knowledge that you will succeed and believe in yourself.

You own the inspirations that will be your main driver, no matter what you face.

You have built up immense courage and belief in yourself.

You know deep down that it's only a matter of time before you hit your goals.

Your inspirations are fuelling your courage – you are moving forward with speed.

This chapter has been, for me, the hardest to write, as it's brought back memories of the most difficult challenges and adversity I have personally faced.

You too may be conjuring up memories that arouse hurt and discomfort, but it's important you stay conscious of these experiences. How you dealt with them, and how you got through, both teach you an immense amount about your character.

Perhaps you've actually looked on this chapter in a more positive light, drawing upon exciting memories, occasions when you excelled through challenge and adversity.

Whatever your perspective on adversity, the fundamental lesson is that adversity teaches you everything you need to know about yourself. It demonstrates to you your capabilities and builds resilience within your mindset.

Never let adversity draw you in as a negative. When adversity strikes, look for immediate positives and ask, 'How can I learn from this?'

ICE reflection 9:
Reflect

As part of this ICE reflection, consider the most intense moment of adversity or hardest challenge you have experienced that jumped out while you read the chapter. It could be the experience you reflected on as part of the earlier exercise or a new one that has come to you later in the chapter.

In your journal, write a short paragraph about how you would deal with that situation again, if you were to experience it once more.

This will help you turn a tough experience into a positive one and grow beyond it so that, should it happen again, you'll be prepared.

The Football Writers' Association Awards

My phone rings out of the blue. It's Terry Byrne, Gareth Southgate's personal manager.

Former physio to the England football team, Terry now runs an extremely successful talent agency in London – 10 Ten Talent – looking after some of the biggest names in football past and present, as well as several other celebrity names.

Terry began managing my sporting hero David Beckham's career after the Manchester United and England star was sent off against Argentina during the 1998 World Cup in France.

Looking after David for many years, Terry managed the superstar's career. Even though Becks has now left the agency, they've remained extremely close pals ever since.

So, given how pivotal he was in my hero's career, you can imagine my elation when I first met Terry. He's a big name in football business. And, somehow, we too have become great friends, with Terry now my closest business mentor.

I answer the phone. 'All right, Tel? How are you, mate?'

'Yeah, good, fella. You?' Terry asks. 'Your family well?'

Tel's a true gentleman, always ensuring everyone is OK before ploughing on with business. I return the courtesy.

'All good, fella,' he continues in his cockney tone. 'Anyway, I've got something for ya.' We're down to business now.

Tel is London through and through, a Chelsea blue at heart. It's where he started his own footballing days many years ago. (He won't mind me saying 'many'!)

'Oh, really? What have you got?' I cautiously respond.

When someone like Terry rings you out of the blue and says they've got something for you, you know it isn't going to be rubbish.

Terry has already hooked our company up with some glittering opportunities, both sporting and business-related, including visiting Manchester United to deliver the ICE model to Manchester United Ladies. He's opening up doors all over the place for us and seems to love doing it.

'What are you doing on 20 Jan.?' he asks me.

It's early October and I haven't planned that far ahead. But, even if I am booked, I will likely go and cancel it if Terry has something for me.

'Not sure, to be honest. How come, mate?' I'm calm. Yet desperate to know what he has.

'Fancy another talking gig, fella?' he continues. 'It's for an awards ceremony.'

Terry pauses, waiting for my reply.

'Err, yes, why not?' I accept, without even knowing what it is I'm agreeing to.

'OK, Gareth is receiving an award from the Football Writers' Association in January for his and England's immense efforts during the World Cup. And we'd like you to deliver the tribute speech for Gareth.'

About thirty seconds pass by before I realize I haven't responded. If only Terry could see me, hanging over my balcony, trying not to lose signal, dressed only in a pair of pants.

'It's a big gig, fella,' he adds. 'Four hundred press, celebrities, sport stars – you name it and they'll be there. Fancy it?'

Tel pauses, then carries on. 'Oh, and it's at the Savoy. So you'll be put up in a room there, all at the expense of the FWA.'

I frown with confusion, as a light cold breeze snaps me out of thought.

'You there, Ben?' Terry prompts.

Shit, have I paused too long? I think to myself. *Have I even got signal?*

I check my screen for reception, but actually to see if I'm dreaming – that Terry really is on the line asking me this.

'Err, yeah . . .' I clear my dry and nervous throat. 'Sorry, yeah, I am here, mate. I would love to.'

Terry continues to deliver the rough outline of the evening – who's going and that my wife and I will be sitting at the top table, with Gareth and his other guests.

And I listen on, with a huge smile wrapped across my face, still dressed in only my underpants.

ENACTMENT

↑

COURAGE

↑

INSPIRATION

10.
Finding the Success You Deserve

WHAT SUCCESS FEELS LIKE FOR ME

I didn't know what success meant to me until I sat down to rousing applause after delivering that speech at the FWA Awards. When Gareth stood to shake my hand and thank me, I suddenly realized how far I had come.

From drug addict to Commando, injured veteran to co-founder of new start-up – every part of my journey had led me to that speech in the Savoy.

For me, that night's success wasn't wrapped up in delivering the speech itself, nor in the celebrity of its recipient. For me, success was comparing the memory of once being on the bones of my arse twelve years prior, to where I was now, standing on that stage with the experience and knowledge I had gathered along the way. And all in front of my wife, who has been by my side the entire journey and gifted me my two wonderful children.

> It was only at the top that I realized what my own success felt like to me. But what does success look like to you?

— Pause for thought —

So let's go back to your journal. I want you to consider the following questions. Think about each one in depth, write a few sentences, or a couple of key words in answer to each question.

- What does the word 'success' mean to you?
- When were you last successful by your definition?
- How do you hold on to success?

YOUR SUCCESS

Everyone's idea of success is different. No two people see success in exactly the same way. Success to you may be to attain great wealth, or to build your perfect family. It may be to complete a lifelong adventure, or to simply live a happy life. Success is what you want it to be, what you decide it is.

In its most basic form, 'success' means to accomplish an aim or purpose, to achieve a desired vision or planned goal. The inspirations you identified at the beginning of this book and then transformed into goals are your targets for success – when you achieve those, in theory you'll have become successful.

Whether you're a parent or teacher, business exec or student, soldier or athlete, you have at some point succeeded; you are all successful. Even purchasing this book has done something to aid your personal growth and design a life you want. Isn't that a really positive sign of success? Wasn't buying and, more importantly, reading the book a small win in itself?

Individual successes can be big or small, but try to view the process of succeeding as an evolutionary cycle, not a one-off achievement. Success needs to be maintained and cannot be left to fend for itself – it's a garden you must tend, demanding lots of hard work to keep it looking good. To be successful, you need to have lots of little wins over time.

FOUR COMMANDO PRINCIPLES TO ACHIEVE SUCCESS

In order to help you be as successful as you can, I want to share four principles for success.

Principle 1: The more you do it, the better you'll become

Exposure = Composure

Ever attended an eye-opening, jaw-dropping motivational talk, where the speaker encapsulates and convinces you that you WILL change, you WILL create a new lease of life for yourself?

Twenty minutes after the speaker left the stage, did you find yourself quickly forgetting large chunks of the talk? Then, a day later, remembering little of it at all? A week on and it was just another speaker, their lessons and message hard to remember, and even harder to incorporate into your life?

It isn't hard in this modern age to quickly forget the inspiring messages and advice we hear and read, before falling back into our normal ways. This isn't because the message wasn't strong. It's because we don't put it into practice.

Sitting back and watching a talk, delving into the latest brilliant personal development book or investing in your own education – it's all fantastic and I encourage you to do as much of it as you can. But it will take more than words and speakers for you to succeed in your goals.

It's going to take time, patience and continuous exposure in several different areas in your life to get better and better at what you do.

You have to take all these messages and lessons, including my own, and actually implement them.

I summarize this with a simple couplet: <u>Exposure = Composure</u>.

Everything you do towards achieving your long-term goals – whether you succeed or fail in the short term – is exposing you to your skills and abilities.

You must want to experience this exposure and urge yourself towards it.

Get your hands dirty

Combat was brutal.

The first time I was engaged, I panicked.

The more it happened and the more we were exposed to the violence of war, the more composed we all became during the most difficult and testing situations.

The training we'd done during the preceding months and years shaped and readied us for what was to come.

About 50 per cent of our initial training consisted of learning the theory and strategy of combat by reading and listening. The rest was physical exercise, and it was this small proportion of time spent training our bodies that turned us into Commandos.

When the tough moments arose in real life, we were better equipped to deal with it and more composed than if we had spent the entirety of the eight months reading material in how to soldier.

Exposure = Composure happens when you get your hands dirty by putting theory into practice.

Now you

Have you followed all the instructions in this book and written out your goals, followed the 'Pause for thought' boxes and completed all the exercises and the ICE reflections?

If you want to achieve anything in life, then you need to step out-side the safety of your comfort zone regularly. If you want to uphold your values, then you must put them into practice. If you want to grow, then exposing yourself to your fears, doubts, fatigue and any adversity you face is how you will succeed.

You can only gain composure, or excellence in your field if you expose yourself to opportunities and put yourself out there.

Remember ICE

As I said at the beginning, this book isn't about getting you cold, wet, muddy and miserable. It's about sharing how a Commando thinks and acts so that you, too, can employ the same strategies and tactics in your own life. The success of your own Commando mindset stems from:

- Knowing what you're working towards and why you're doing it – <u>YOUR INSPIRATION</u>.
- Understanding your body's neurological and adrenal responses, harnessing fear and growing belief – <u>YOUR COURAGE</u>.
- Daring to take steps, not procrastinating, owning an ability to overcome adversity and keep going – <u>YOUR ENACTMENT</u>.

However, you aren't going to learn a single thing about yourself until you practise what is preached.

Principle 2: Concentrate only on what you can control

In *The 7 Habits of Highly Effective People*, Stephen Covey uses a simple model, the 'circle of influence', to illustrate what is in a person's con-trol and what isn't (see diagram overleaf).

In order to succeed, it's important you learn to recognize whether you can control something or not so that you don't waste energy try-ing to manipulate what you can't change or influence.

Is what you worry about within your control, or outside it?

Many of the thoughts that cross our mind every day – your

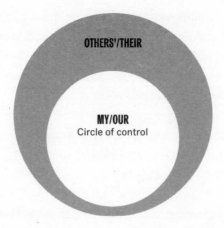

boss's bad mood, the weather, the traffic jam, your competitor's new funding – are all out of your control.

If you lack control over something, then you must let it go, no matter how hard that may seem. Focus on what you can control instead, your own thoughts, actions, plans, efforts, mistakes, behaviour.

Inside your circle of control, you can control and effectively implement the ICE model. You can grasp your inspirations, grow your courage and take steps towards enacting what you have planned. You control your destiny and are the only one accountable for everything within the circle.

Outside the circle are other people's words, actions, thoughts, failings and feelings. Granted, some of these areas you may be able to have an effect on, but at what cost to yourself?

Control where you're stepping

Knowing how high the IED threat was when we first deployed to Afghanistan, I found myself taking an age to walk even a few steps, worried in case the ground violently erupted around me, taking my limbs with it.

With graphic images of amputees and mutilated bodies clouding my mind, I was concerned about every foot placement.

However, once I was able to accept what was within my control and what was not, I could operate and function more effectively. We all could.

I knew the Taliban had hidden the bombs; I knew they were hidden extremely well and very difficult to identify; I had no control over either of those factors.

But, inside my circle, I had control over my diligence and an ability to recognize the ground signs ('combat indicators of IEDs') and the most likely areas for their placement, giving me the best opportunity in identifying and/or avoiding them.

When we went out on an operation, I had zero control over when or where the enemy would shoot at us, but I owned full control over how I would react and respond, as did my friends.

We'd have been wasting our time with the 'what if's, so the best course of action was to stay focused on what we controlled – ourselves.

Now you

In the last chapter, I emphasized that adversity in one way or another is bound to strike you at some point. There's little chance of you achieving your goals without adversity rearing its head. The more audacious your goals, the more likely adversity is to occur. But adversity is out of your control and looms outside your circle; you must concentrate on what is inside.

There will be precautionary and preventative measures you can take to minimize adversity's impact, but you can't sit around worrying and waiting for it – this will simply eat away at you.

You must concentrate on staying focused and ensuring you do not become distracted by what's outside your circle of control.

Soon, you'll be snapping shut this book. You will, once again, be alone.

Be prepared for challenge and adversity, but neither avoid nor concern yourself over them.

Cast little doubt or worry over what *might* happen.

Stay focused on what you know you can influence.

To mitigate your existing worries and repel further intrusive ones, consider this process created by Dale Carnegie:

1. Ask yourself, what is the worst that could happen?
2. Accept that this either will or will not happen.
3. Then try to make the worst part better.

— Pause for thought —

Draw a circle using a teacup to create your own circle of control.

Within this circle, list everything relevant that is in your control, mindful of your inspirations and goals.

Now use a bowl to draw a bigger circle around your first one. In this outer circle, list all the things that are outside your control.

When you've finished this exercise, pin up both this piece of paper and your goals somewhere prominent to remind you what you can focus on and which thoughts or worries out of your control you need to leave behind.

Principle 3: Never give up

Richard Branson came close to bankruptcy on several occasions before founding Virgin. Sir James Dyson had 5,126 failed prototypes over fifteen years. And J. K. Rowling was a jobless, divorced parent, and as poor as it is possible to be without being homeless. Later, as one of the world's most successful women, she was able to say as part of her inspiring speech at Harvard in 2008:

'It is impossible to live without failing at something, unless you live so cautiously that you might as well not have lived at all – in which case, you fail by default.'

What all of these people have in common was that they kept going, they never lost their motivation and belief in themselves or their ideas.

Now you

You may be many months away from success, or you could be on the cusp of it. Whatever stage you're at, your motivation will be the main attribute that will get you there.

Anything you face, good or bad, you can battle through if you keep your motivation in play; it is your ally for success. The Commando mindset is underpinned by motivation and it's going to help you do whatever it takes to achieve the success you desire.

I asked you at the beginning of this book to write down inspirations and goals that light a fire within you, ones that will encourage you to keep going. When your motivation is tested, you'll quickly find out if you have picked the right inspirations or not, so be clear in what you want. You have to stay motivated if you want to succeed – it's a must!

If you follow the guidelines in this book and remember the ICE model in your day-to-day life, you'll open up wonderful opportunities that may once not have been there, and dramatically improve your potential for success.

Principle 4: Always have your blinkers off

Never over, always beginning

When I found out my career in the Royal Marines was over as a result of hearing impairment, I was devastated and shocked. Yet I immediately had to begin looking outside the military to see what I would be able to do next. Speaking, consulting and coaching became my trade of choice.

At once I began harnessing all my existing skills and applying them to my new ventures. I'd spent the last ten years leading and being led. Deciding I no longer wanted to work within a hierarchical structure, I resolved to build my own empire, and that I would never work for anyone again. This is where my entrepreneurial career began.

Do it anyway

I knew nothing about business, zilch!

Through family and friends, my only understanding of being in business was failure.

Everyone close to me who had ever started up a company or taken one over had, in the end, failed.

And there I was, replacing weapons and camouflage with pens and paper, without a clue what I was doing.

VAT and tax, budgets, domain names, quotes and invoices, spreadsheets, accountants and solicitors, investment was a whole new language to me.

I swiftly learned that parts of my military bearing would carry me a very short distance.

It turns out that shouting at potential clients and telling them to do press-ups isn't effective.

Few people in business seemed interested in my military background.

I had to step into a whole new world, one where I would need to learn everything again if I was to make it.

My first web designer was Steve – a close friend who had been in business most of his life. He sat me down and advised me how I should tackle my new career; he also warned me of the pitfalls and the immense risk I was opening myself up to. He gave me a realistic perspective and laid out the steps he had taken to become successful himself.

I soaked up every word like a sponge. I knew what I wanted to do and was primed to go. At the end of our meeting, he parted on a few words that have always stuck with me and are the reason for many of my successes since: 'Always have your blinkers off.'

Steve was encouraging me always to be open to learning new things and to seek opportunity where I wouldn't necessarily have done. He was encouraging me to adopt the mindset of an entrepreneur.

Now you

A year from now, your inspirations and goals may have changed. Your life may be heading in a different direction, away from where you first intended. You could find yourself reaching for very different things. Take comfort in knowing that situations and scenarios will evolve. Allow yourself comfort in thinking you can do what you want, even if it's something entirely new.

Remember:

- Have the blinkers off and look around you, observe what others are doing and new trends.
- Be willing to search different fields and discover new paths.
- Ensure your skills are being channelled into the correct avenues. Could they be better positioned?
- Ask yourself whether you are truly satisfied with your current position. If not, how could you change it?

Having the blinkers off doesn't mean being unfocused. It means always being aware what's happening around you while also being focused. Having your blinkers off will leave you open to new experiences and lessons, ready to move to the place that will let you be your best and do your best.

NOW IS YOUR TIME

Everything in this book is aimed at arming you with the tools that will force you to focus and drive towards success. The exercises and reflections will have made you consider and analyse many aspects of your life in real detail.

To get through this book you've probably thought about some of the following: money, career, health, family, friends and difficult memories. This in itself will have been highly demanding. Getting through that may have been very difficult for you. But it's a testament to your character.

You are a unique and valuable individual who owns unimaginable potential. You have the world before you. All you need to do now is step into it.

One of the things we find hardest in life is getting going. It is so easy to dream and live the life you want within your head, but doing it in reality is a very different story. I believe you can do it. Now you're equipped with the Commando mindset, it's time you went out and got whatever it is that you want.

After possibly years of thinking about it, now is the time to start doing and to make something more of your dreams. In order to enact, all you need to do is action the plan you created around your goals.

Cognitive behavioural therapy expert David D. Burns states: 'Motivation does not come first, action does.' Waiting for that sudden moment of motivation won't get you very far. Do not wait around for the 'right' time to do something: it'll never come. Start acting now, and the motivation will naturally flow.

Commando Mindset has, I hope, helped you unearth or rediscover your inspirations and goals. Your motivation will stem from your engagement with those goals. So, what are you waiting for? Let's start working towards those dreams and ambitions!

ICE reflection 10:
What is your remaining battery life?

As of September 2018, according to the UK's Office for National Statistics, British women have an average life expectancy of 82.9 years, with men at 79.3.

So, praying you live towards these figures without any life-ending tragedies along the way, the final exercise towards achieving the Commando mindset is to calculate your remaining battery life using the following:

Your age in years and months (e.g. 31.7) x 100, divided by your life expectancy (82.9 for women or 79.3 for men). Round up if your month figure is 10 or more.

The answer is your used battery life in a percentage.

At the time of writing, mine is 40 per cent used up. I'm not going to let another day go by without doing that extra bit more.

How much of your battery life is used up? Write it down in your journal.

Life is a brief, one-shot opportunity to flourish at something.

So, how much more of your battery will you let die before you make a move on what it is you want to achieve?

Many of you will already have incredible achievements in your life, things you should be immensely proud of.

But no matter how much battery you've used, you still have ample time to do a bit more of the cool stuff – achieving your dreams.

YOUR STORY

If one advances confidently in the direction of his dreams, and endeavours to live the life which he has imagined, he will meet a success unexpected in common hours.

Henry David Thoreau

What doesn't kill you makes you stronger

As worried, apprehensive faces begin entering the wood, I'm doing my utmost to control my excited smile. International football stars are approaching. Just as nervous of me as I am of them.

'Right, grab your fucking kit and hurry up!' bellows the voice of Sergeant Taff Prosser in his distinctive Welsh accent.

'HURRY UP, THEN, YOU LOT! START MOVING YOUR FINGERS.' All five of us corporals join in.

I can't help but chuckle inside. Harry Kane is frantically looking for the kit with his name on. Panicking, helplessly seeking his camouflage bergen in among everyone else's. They're all running round like headless chickens.

'Get a grip of yourself and find your kit, KANE!' Danny yells, trying to cover up his smirk with a steely look.

We're having fun. It's an opportunity we're not likely to get again. Yelling at talented superstars who at this moment resemble rabbits in headlights more than professional footballers.

'OI, SOUTHGATE!' Taff yells again. 'Get your kit and fall in line like the rest.' My sergeant looks over at me with a cheeky wink. 'Hurry up, then!' he enforces, still grinning.

Actually, this is as serious for us as it is for the players. But it's an opportunity we can't miss – giving the superstars a taste of our life.

They've not been in our presence for more than an hour before we're handing out paintball guns and minimal protective equipment. Leading them off to an attack against highly trained Royal Marines recruits. Then a night under the stars.

Once the dust settles and the players and staff find their feet, we drop the Commando exterior and begin interacting with them like normal people – the ice is broken. They want to know about us and our world as much as we want to know about theirs.

I'm pinching myself, sitting opposite our nation's skipper late at night. A young man I've watched excel through his football career now sits opposite in an orange ambient glow. Yet there's no awkwardness. We're just talking openly, person to person, not marine to player.

In fact, I get so deeply lost in the conversation that I begin dripping about holiday prices – how it's just cost me over £2,000 to take the family away to Lanzarote. I'm only briefly forgetting that Harry Kane would pay a lot more for the places he visits. Yet, ever the professional, he agrees and we continue our chat.

I ask him the obligatory questions: 'What does it feel like to score in front of 80,000 fans at Wembley?' 'What's it like to take a penalty?' With grace, Harry answers each one for the millionth time.

But he's also eager to know about life in the marines, quickly switching to Afghanistan, questioning me on what it's like to experience combat.

His questions provoke a more formal and direct answer from me. I realize that this is what the players are here for, to understand with a whole new perspective what it takes to experience adversity and challenge. If I can help them in even the tiniest way, then I'll happily share my story with the England captain.

Speaking for another hour or so, I let him know the details of combat and what my friends and I experienced on operations.

Harry takes it all in. Suddenly, the roles and admiration have flipped. He's lapping up every word I say.

'That must have been horrific going through that,' Harry wonders. I have to pause and think.

'Yeah, I suppose so. But what doesn't kill you makes you stronger,' I reply.

Harry absorbs this. I pass him back the cup of tea we're sharing.

I'm thinking, *Always have the blinkers off and look around. Watch how other people deal with the troubles that life throws at us all.*

I know Harry will take away some of what I'm saying to help himself and the squad. I know 'what doesn't kill you makes you stronger' strikes a chord with the England front man.

However, I'm also learning a great deal from Harry.

I can finally understand the coping methods he uses to deal with his own pressures of playing for club and country. And how any unfortunate slip of the tongue in an interview, or poor touch of the ball, can lead to millions of people ridiculing him and his family.

I take from him as much as he takes from me. That's what we should all do, constantly learn from other people's resilience and character.

During a moment of silence, I find myself once more thinking of the explosion that took out my patrol, about my brothers who were devastatingly injured. Even sitting in a wood with the England captain, the realities of war can swiftly command your attention.

For so long, that explosion has plagued me as a negative incident that deeply affected all of us. Yet, here I am, now telling the tale to help our England captain lead our nation's team into a World Cup.

For the first time, I'm witnessing how the impact of my fellow marines and me can be made applicable to those outside the military, to build their own resilience.

'My military career is coming to an end. I wonder if I can do what I'm doing now as a career – coaching and helping professionals find their upper edge?' I say to myself.

YOUR STORY

11.
Summarizing the
Commando Mindset

IF I CAN DO IT, SO CAN YOU

In 2016, when I sat down behind my dated laptop in a small and cold understairs cupboard, I could never have imagined writing *Commando Mindset*.

I first began writing this book as a journal and memoir of everything I had been through, to free my mind from intrusive thoughts and dark memories; but as I began writing it, I realized that I wasn't writing down what was hurting me, but instead what had helped me get through it all.

I wasn't purging myself of dark thoughts, but confronting them and realizing what processes had helped me get to where I am. About two chapters in, I knew this book could be more than a memoir, it could be a book to help others in their own quest for success.

Forty-eight months later, *Commando Mindset* can be found in bookshops all over the world.

The reason I'm telling you this is to demonstrate that if I can do it, so can you. If a low-life, suicidal drug addict, stuck within a perpetual cycle of crime, violence, depression and desperation, can break free, transform his life and realize his dreams, you can as well.

You can do anything you set your mind to. You just need to have the determination and courage to follow through on your dreams.

THE ICE MODEL – YOUR RECIPE FOR SUCCESS

As I said at the start, you *already* use the ICE model within your life. You *are* already inspired by something – maybe many things – and there are several reasons why you get out of bed each morning. However, up until this point you may have been focusing on them in the wrong way.

Equipped with a Commando mindset and the ICE model, you can forge a new path, pick new inspirations and goals, and live out the one and only life you have to its fullest.

I don't just preach the ICE model, but live by it, too. Over the years my business partner Tommo and I have used it continuously. It has become the backbone of every coaching session, talk or workshop we deliver. We also use the ICE model within our own lives, every day, constantly working on old and new inspirations and striving to succeed at them.

The ICE model is simple yet impactful. If you own it in the same way I do, I've no doubt you'll go on to achieve remarkable things.

Before I draw *Commando Mindset* to a close – let's make a final recap of the ICE model, highlighting the key areas in which you can implement it and reminding ourselves of how the traffic-light system helps us get ready to go.

INSPIRATION (THE RED LIGHT)

- Everything begins with a vision, a picture, a dream, a desire to achieve; we call these <u>Inspirations</u>.
- Your inspirations are your red traffic light. Stop. Consider. Choose your inspirations wisely.

- Ensure that what you aim for fills you with excitement and that you're doing it for yourself, not anyone else.
- Transform your inspirations into small, clearly defined goals that relate to your overall ambition.
- Write down your goals and put them where you can see them every day to continually remind yourself of what it is you're doing and why.
- Break the journey down with deadlines for the completion of each step – and register every win and success.
- Your personal values are the backbone of your inspirations.
- Every decision you make when considering your inspirations should align with your personal values.
- A Commando mindset means being prepared to live and die according to a set of values, values that guide you through uncertainty, helping you make decisions with integrity.
- Be willing to step outside your comfort zone and embrace challenge.
- Whenever times turn bleak, look back at your inspirations and remind yourself why you are doing what you are doing, then be ready to go again.

COURAGE (THE AMBER LIGHT)

- Courage is your bridge between dreaming (inspiration) and doing (enactment).
- To achieve anything, you must first believe. Build the courage and belief you need to go on and achieve your goals.
- Make fear your friend and see it as a positive feeling – it primes and readies you, heightens your senses, makes you more determined and teaches you your own true capabilities.
- Surround yourself with excellence and people who will support you in your quest.

- Your community and network will either make or break you.
- The people you need to be around are those of an equally infectious and positive mindset, and who are equally or even more driven than you are.
- If you are the most successful person in the room, you need to change rooms.
- Learn from those who have achieved what you aspire to and ensure you're always learning from those around you.
- Always be learning and growing, including during difficulty and challenge.
- Never get comfortable – be willing to test yourself, learning from every mistake and failure, win and success. Each of your actions, whether successes or failures, should be deemed as a positive step forward.
- Take small steps at first and test the waters of your comfort zone before building confidence and momentum, tackling larger and larger challenges as you progress.
- When you're faced with a challenge, setback or obstacle, take a Condor moment and remember why you're doing what you are doing.
- Remind yourself of your inspirations and goals.

ENACTMENT (THE GREEN LIGHT)

- <u>Enactment</u> is the leap of faith you need to take.
- Your inspirations are now goals. You are primed with courage and belief. All that's now required is for you to enact everything you have planned.
- Be prepared to get shit done and do not allow yourself to fall into the bad habit of procrastinating.
- Owning a Commando mindset means you must always be willing to go that extra step further then everyone else, which means never putting things off.

- Stay acutely aware of laziness and make a conscious effort to always do the things you don't feel like doing – this includes taking that first step, now.
- See positivity in everything that you do, and ensure every win or loss, setback or success is viewed with a positive perspective.
- Celebrate the small wins and recognize every single achievement, relishing the pleasure chemicals you are rewarded with every time you achieve something.
- Be ready to face adversity head-on – the adversity you face and your ability to deal with it will turn you into a far more resilient character. Learn and grow with it.
- Adversity will often seem as if it is trying to put you off your goals. Try to see the positive in anything it brings.
- Adversity is not an enemy; it's an asset that teaches you about yourself.
- Remember who you are and what you're doing it all for.
- Your inspirations are your strength, your courage is your weapon; use them to your advantage.
- If you fall off the wagon, get straight back on it.
- Rebuild your courage by reminding yourself of your inspirations.
- If your journey is difficult it's probably because you're doing something right – testing and challenging yourself.
- Define what success means for you.
- Use past successes to keep you motivated.
- Keep the blinkers off, and grow your courage and belief even more; they are formed by the success you feed them with.

GOOD LUCK

Your journal, which I hope is looking a bit tired and scribbled in by now, is your reminder of everything you have covered in this book. Within its pages are some of your deepest thoughts, reflections and ambitions that you may not have shared with anyone before. Treasure this journal as the blueprint for your future success.

Remember, when you feel like stopping, when you feel like quitting, DON'T. Accept the pain and discomfort; fear and trepidation are indicators that you're heading in the right direction. Embrace them.

Keep in touch

It may take me a day or two to respond, maybe even a couple of months, but please do get in touch if you've found *Commando Mindset* and the ICE model helpful or have any questions. I promise I'll get back to you.

You can email me at ben@findyouredgecoaching.com, hit me up on Instagram (@ben_williams_cm), or find me on LinkedIn. I'd love to hear how you're getting on with the ICE model and how *Commando Mindset* has helped you.

If you'd like to hear more about what I am doing and attend our courses and workshops, or to book me to speak at one of your events, then email my team at info@findyouredgecoaching.com or visit www.findyouredgecoaching.com, putting as the subject 'courses and workshop' or 'speaking enquiry'.

At our public events you'll have the opportunity to meet other extraordinary people just like you who are applying ICE and the Commando mindset within their own lives, and to surround yourself with excellence. If you can't get enough of the ICE model and think you would like to help teach it to other great people and share your own story, then email info@findyouredgecoaching.com with the subject 'inspire others'.

PREPARE TO MOVE

Every time you go firm (i.e. stop moving) on patrol, before starting off again, the order will be given: 'Prepare to move.'

On this command, you get your last chance to check your weapon, ensure the pouches of your equipment are shut, look around – especially towards where you're moving. Check your buddies are good to go, then move off on the command: 'Move!'

'Is my weapon ready to fire?'
'Where are the likely enemy firing points?'
'Is my equipment in order?'
'Do I know the mission?'
'Is there enough ammunition in my magazine, or shall I change it?'
'I need to check on the other guys.'
'It's time to go . . .'

Now you

Now, it's you who's about to move out.

Everything in this book is your equipment checklist, ready for the task ahead – you're preparing to move.

'Am I passionate about my inspirations?'
'Are my goals tangible and strategically planned?'
'Are my values and beliefs in check?'
'Is my courage primed?'
'Am I ready to enact?'

You are about to step foot on your patrol.

Now is the final moment to ensure you're good to go.

Check yourself off, believe you can do this, be ready for the mission.

'*Prepare to move . . .*'

'*. . . Move!*'

FURTHER READING

Stephen R. Covey, *The 7 Habits of Highly Effective People* (Free Press, 1989)

Carol S. Dweck, *Mindset: Changing the Way You Think to Fulfil Your Potential* (Robinson, 2017)

Susan Jeffers, *Feel the Fear and Do It Anyway: How to Turn Your Fear and Indecision into Confidence and Action* (Vermilion, 2007)

Gail Matthews, Goals Research Study, Dominican University of California, 2007; https://www.dominican.edu/academics/lae/undergraduate-programs/psych/faculty/assets-gail-matthews/researchsummary2.pdf

Cal Newport, *Digital Minimalism: Choosing a Focused Life in a Noisy World* (Penguin, 2019)

Mel Robbins, *The 5 Second Rule: The Surprisingly Simple Way to Live, Love, and Speak with Courage: Transform your Life, Work, and Confidence with Everyday Courage* (Post Hill Press, 2017)

Simon Sinek, *Leaders Eat Last: Why Some Teams Pull Together and Others Don't* (Penguin, 2014)

Robert J. Vallerand, *The Psychology of Passion: A Dualistic Model* (Oxford University Press, 2015)

Bronnie Ware, *The Top Five Regrets of the Dying: A Life Transformed by the Dearly Departing* (Hay House, 2012)

ACKNOWLEDGEMENTS

Commando Mindset would simply not have been possible without the aid of so many influential people from across all parts of my life. I have written out lists and lists of names that I feel indebted to. However, the number of people who have helped and supported me on my journey would fill another two hundred pages; whittling it down to the following names and words has been as tough as writing the book! Even if your name isn't here, please understand that every single one of you has played a role in making me who I am, and I can't thank you enough.

There is no better place to start than Mum, Dad and Denise, my stepmother. It has been a rollercoaster journey for us all, and, like any family, we have experienced the highs and lows of life. We have all had our own problems, but I can't thank you enough for sticking by me when I have been at my lowest, highest and most difficult, often putting my problems before your own. You have all taught me so much over the years and, unbeknown to you all, I probably would not be here writing these words if it wasn't for your undying trust and support.

Mum, you personally deserve a special mention. Since life took a dramatic turn for us all many years ago, you, without hesitation and no matter what adversity you faced, ensured you always put Josh and me before anything else. I know you sometimes question the difficult decisions you had to make, and whether they were the right ones for my brother and me. Let me use this opportunity to ensure you that *every* single decision you made was correct. Life would not be how it is now without those decisions, and I am forever grateful for your ability to face fear and always do the right thing. If there is anyone who epitomizes the Commando mindset, it's you. Mum, you own the courage, tenacity and integrity equal to that of any of my brothers in arms. But you have also taught me compassion, empathy and, most importantly, the art of forgiveness. You raised us beyond expectations.

Though we sometimes have our differences in opinion, Josh, you have always stuck by me. Keep that drive and ambition you now own and ensure you make the absolute most of your life. You will always be my little brother and, like you have supported me, I will forever support you. Keep smashing it.

Aunty Suzy, there are few words I can write that would justify how much you mean to me. At my lowest, your voice of wisdom helped me realize the changes I needed to make, and showed me what I was capable of, without ever asking for anything in return. You always put others before yourself, which is why you own such a warm place in everyone's heart.

I would never have stepped out into the realms of uncertainty without the encouragement and support of my friends back home. Yes, we did things we shouldn't have, and often got one another into a lot of trouble. Granted, we were once rather naughty, and spent many an evening locked up in cold cells, and for that we remain a tight group that has forged unbreakable bonds. Hen, Paul, Sharpy, Luke, Rob, Gibby, Tommy and Gianni, thanks for bailing me out on more than one occasion. But most importantly, thanks for being the handful of people who believed I could change and follow my ambitions, escaping who I was becoming.

Jason, when you said the words at my wedding, 'I don't know how you picked me as a best man, as there is a table full of them over there,' you were right; it was a difficult task to choose. But there is a reason I picked you, and I can't thank you enough for always being there for my family, children and me. You are everything a best man should be, which is why you had the important role on the day.

Ten years of my life have been spent among the finest and most exceptional group of people, the Royal Marines Commandos. From the lowest lows to the highest highs, every single marine I came across taught me something new. Most importantly, the marines I spent my time with always taught me to exceed my own expectations every day, even if it was only by a small amount. Such people encouraged me to be the best version of myself, no matter what I faced, which still stands to this very day.

The Royal Marines is a unique environment, full of incredible people who always go that bit further for one another. Someone once asked me what I miss most about the Royal Marines. I miss the people within it. I miss the organization where the culture is the centre of everything and underpins almost every decision. I hope every organization can one day have a culture like that of the Royal Marines. An organization so incredibly humbling to be part of; it still makes the hairs on my neck stand up when I say I served as a Commando.

Lima Company, 42 Commando, is where it all began. The warriors I fought side by side with on operations exemplified what it meant to be a Royal Marine in battle. It was you guys who showed me that it was never acceptable to hide in the face of danger, and always to confront the fears that stare back at you. Every single one of you committed actions that deemed the highest recognition and witnessed horrific moments in battle. Yet every single one of you stands tall and proud within the shadows, never shouting about what you did, and staying humble to who you are.

Vicey, Ben, Gaz, Damo, Matt, Jake, Darlo, Loz, Richy, Frenchy, Dave, Ash, Joe, Tommo, Mike, Jord and all the rest: you own the hearts of lions. Thank you for guiding me through such uncertain times, and for being the ones who would courageously stand at my shoulder when I needed protecting.

As my military career began its ending, I needed to think on my feet and trust myself in what I wanted to do. To my last Commando training team, Richy, Matt, Danny, Taff and Charlie, thank you so much for inspiring me to write this book, and for giving me so much time off when I needed to concentrate on building my new life.

Part of this journey would never have existed had I not had the good fortune to meet and work with Harry Kane and Gareth Southgate – acknowledgements I never thought I would ever make. I want to thank you both for giving me opportunities I could only have dreamed of as a young boy. The moments you granted me may seem minimal to you, but they mean the world to me. Equally, Mr Terry Byrne, you have humbled me with your generosity and support, and I'm so pleased to call you a friend.

A special mention to those who brought this book together. To Nick Walters, my agent: your belief in and vision for *Commando Mindset* were unrivalled. I can't thank you enough for seeing so much in this project, and for willingly stepping away from your normal genres and having faith in me. To Lydia Yadi, my editor: I also owe you such a special thanks for believing in this book. Though it has had many forms and evolved a lot over the last year, you stuck with me and have been so receptive to my ideas. I also owe you a great big thank you for diluting my swearing and some abrasive comments, while maintaining the impact I so wanted to make. Special mention to Martina, Matt, Leo, Celia, Ellie, Trevor and the wider Penguin team who have come together to make this book a reality. A HUGE thank you to Mark Griffiths, who helped me piece *Commando Mindset* together, and for bringing it to life. You too have been incredible to work with, and I know this is only the start of our writing journey together.

Angie Sage and husband Rhodri, your brilliant writing careers and experience provided me with so much direction, and your advice has been priceless. Thank you for spending hours with my manuscript during its infancy, and for caring about my writing journey so much.

Thank you to Antony, my business partner, for building and sharing this new life with me so far. Together we are building the businesses we have both always dreamed of, all the while staying true to what we believe in. Good effort for putting up with me so far on our long journeys, but they are only going to get worse. Also, please stop wearing your bright orange cord trousers to meetings.

I must give a very special mention to my wife's parents, Tony and Linda. When I first met you both, I decided it would be a good idea to try to do a kickflip on my skateboard, right next to your brand-new glass front door. I'm sorry for not landing the stunt, and in turn smashing the entire door as my board flew out from under my feet. However, even though my extreme-sports skills didn't impress, you took me in like I was one of your own. Being a father now to a little girl, I now know why Tony was so tough on me when it came to dating Natalie; you had every right to treasure her, and I can't thank you enough for finally allowing me to marry your daughter. I hope I did you proud.

And so, to my darling wife. Like every other couple, we have had our fair share of ups and downs, trials and tribulations, and, at times, been on and off more than Ross and Rachel from *Friends*; yet you still stuck by and always believed in me. From elaborate ideas like when I told you I was going to invent a handbag with an alarm on to stop thieves (I still think it's a good idea) to waving goodbye before I flew out to Afghanistan, you always encouraged me. You are the person who did the most to help me avoid prison, escape my darker life and reinvent myself as a marine. You stuck by me during war and my career, and now during my newest ventures. Your belief in me is unflinching and I can't thank you enough, but never forget to reward yourself with some of your own belief – you are far more capable than you think.

My life changed for ever when you brought the first and then the second of our beautiful children into this world – my utter everythings for whom I do, and would do, anything. Kids, when you are finally able to read and understand this book, I want you to remember how precious your lives are, and make every effort to live the best life possible.

Zachary, my son, you are turning into one of the most decent human beings I have ever had the privilege of being around, and if I could be half the man you are, I would be an extremely happy one. You are a credit to yourself, and I am so proud of who you have become and where you are going. Keep being who you are, and never change your outlook on life; it is beyond admirable.

Layla, what can I say? For the first year and a half I wondered what the hell we had given birth to. Tantrums, screaming and very long nights were not uncommon, and I owned visions of you one day running a cartel or prison gang, rather than living a normal life. But now, I simply realize that you were trying to communicate with the world in your own little way. You are a far cry from then, now a polite and very mature miniprincess, and you have your daddy wrapped around your pinkie. However, I want you to promise one little thing to me, and that is to just slow down growing up for a minute, and stay who you are a little longer.

As a word of warning to Layla's future partner: you need not worry about the immense number of dangerous characters I mention within this book who still protect Layla to this day. It is Layla you need to be scared of, and I commend that person who one day decides to marry her. Good luck!

I also want to mention several people who, I'm sad to say, will never get to read this book. To Frank and Nanny Bet Bet, not only were you the best possible grandparents to Natalie and her brother Daniel, but you equally made me feel as much part of your family as your own grandchildren. Frank, I still polish my boots now, and, I'm sorry, but I'm back to shaving my head and looking like a billiard ball. To Uncle Martin, who felt trapped inside a person you thought you hated, we never judged you, and everyone loved you for who you were, and I hope you are far happier now, wherever you are. Aunty Audrey and Grandma Moira, you have been my guiding lights, but now I ask you to guide my own children for me, and ensure you do whatever it was that you did for me. Aunty Babs, you were and still are my biggest fan. I hope I've made you proud, and I'm sure you and your brother, Uncle Malcolm, now watch over us all with big smiles on your faces.

Deano, you were a young warrior who laid down his life for those around him. Every marine who knew you still talks with unbounded pride about having had the immense privilege to have served with you. You epitomized a Royal Marine and did everything right.

Towards the end of writing *Commando Mindset*, in November 2019, my dear uncle Adrian Payne unexpectedly passed away at fifty-six. He was an incredible man with a passion for putting everyone else first. Payne, as he was known to his family and friends, owned a smile that would light up any room, and an infectious laugh which boomed above any sound. He leaves behind his wife Jo, and children Henry, Millie, Alfie and Maddie. But as Henry said on the day after his father's death, 'We will be fine, he built an incredible team here,' my young cousin's words epitomizing his positive perspective on adversity. These acknowledgements got that little bit harder to write when Payne passed, and so it is an utter privilege to dedicate this book to Adrian, along with my family.

Lastly, I want to thank you, the reader. I am so grateful to you for picking this book up and choosing me as someone you would like to read about and learn from. Each and every one of you has a story to tell, and knows people equal to those I have mentioned here. Be sure to tell those people you love them and care for them, encourage each and every one to go out into the world with courage and determination.

Go and live your best life!

In Memory of the Magnificent Seven killed on Operation Herrick 14, 2011

Marine Nigel Dean Mead, KIA 15 May 2011, aged 19
Marine Sam Alexander, KIA 27 May 2011, aged 28
Lieutenant Ollie Augustin, KIA 27 May 2011, aged 23
Lance Corporal Martin Gill, KIA 5 June 2011, aged 22
Marine James Wright, KIA 5 August 2011, aged 22
Sergeant Barry Weston, KIA 30 August 2011, aged 40
Marine David Fairbrother, KIA 19 September 2011, aged 24

Never below us,
Never above us,
Always by our side.